★ HIGHEST SCORES ★ BEST TIMES
★ AMAZING FEATS ★ BIGGEST GAMES

ALL-TIME GAMING RECORDS

ALL-TIME GAMING RECORDS

EDITOR-IN-CHIEF
Jon White

EDITOR
Luke Albigés

CONTRIBUTORS
Jon Denton, Ross Hamilton, Dom Peppiatt, Drew Sleep, Josh West

HEAD OF DESIGN
Greg Whitaker

LEAD DESIGNER
Adam Markiewicz

DESIGNERS
Steve Mumby, Newton Ribeiro, Will Shum

PRODUCTION
Sarah Bankes, Sarah MacLeod, Jen Neal, Rachel Terzian

All statistics, facts, and other information in this book are accurate
at the time of going to press. Some record-breaking games that feature
M-rated (mature) content have been omitted, all the records featured
here are for games that you can play.

The publisher does not have any control over and does not assume any
responsibility for author or third party websites or their content,
including the websites of any brands, gamers, and social media
personalities included in this book.

Great gaming rivals Mario and Sonic first appeared in the same game in 2007, settling their differences on the sports field in *Mario & Sonic at the Olympic Games!*

HEAD-TO-HEAD HEROES!

STAYING SAFE AND HAVING FUN

Video games are amazing, but it's important that you know how to play safely and responsibly, especially in the competitive world of setting and breaking records. Follow these ten simple tips to get the most out of your gaming experience.

1 Discuss and agree rules with your parents regarding how long you can play for at a time, what websites you can visit on the Internet, and what apps and games you can use.

2 Remember to take frequent breaks during gaming sessions.

3 If you start to get frustrated with a game, level, or boss, take a break and do something else. You'll do better when you return to it fresh!

4 Record every record attempt—you don't want to lose a great run!

5 Tell your parents or a teacher if you come across anything online that makes you feel uncomfortable, upset, or scared.

6 Try not to be overly competitive. Record-breaking communities are typically full of friendly, helpful people, so try to offer others the kind of support you'd like to receive.

7 Pay attention to age ratings on games. They exist for a reason—to help protect you from any content that's not right for you, not to stop you having fun!

8 Don't download or install software or apps to any device, or fill out any forms on the Internet, without checking with the person who owns the device you're using first.

9 Focusing on a single game is the best way to improve, but don't be afraid to move on if you get bored. Games are supposed to be fun, after all!

10 When using streaming services, always check with an adult before changing to a different channel, video, or game.

CONTENTS

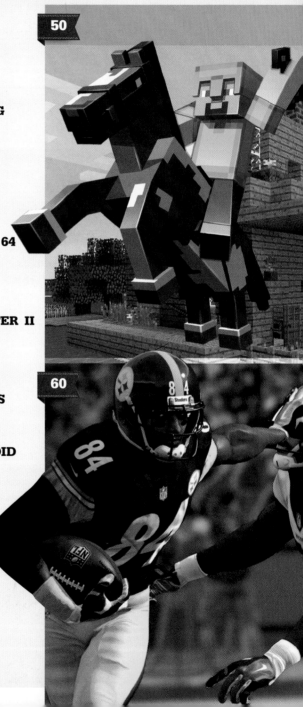

8-17 THE BIGGEST GAMES EVER!
The franchises that conquered the gaming world

18-19 HALL OF FAME: PAC-MAN
The greatest feats of gaming's hungriest star

20-29 PLATFORMERS
Meet the masters of Mario and Sonic's superstars

30-39 ROLE-PLAYING GAMES
Epic adventures mastered in minutes!

40-41 HALL OF FAME: DONKEY KONG
Barrels of amazing arcade facts!

42-49 ACHIEVEMENTS & TROPHIES
Awesome accolades and the greatest gamers!

50-57 MINECRAFT
It's nowhere near as simple as it looks . . .

58-59 PERFECT RUNS
Scores and times that are impossible to beat

60-67 SPORTS GAMES
Introducing the world's best digital athletes

68-69 HALL OF FAME: SUPER MARIO 64
How Mario changed 3-D gaming forever

70-75 GAMING TREASURES
The rarest games of all time

76-83 ADVENTURE GAMES
Gaming's boldest explorers set forth

84-85 HALL OF FAME: STREET FIGHTER II
Looking back at the record-breaking fighter

86-89 HARDWARE HEAVEN
The best (and worst) tech the world has ever seen

90-93 MULTIPLAYER GAMES
Making short work of the competition

94-95 THE BIGGEST GAMING EVENTS
Bringing gamers together in record numbers!

96-101 INDIE GAMES
Who doesn't love a good underdog story?

102-103 HALL OF FAME: SUPER METROID
The adventure that created a genre

104-107 THE CRAZIEST RECORDS
OF ALL TIME
The lengths to which some players will go . . .

108-113 RACING GAMES
Tearing through the pack like a Blue Shell!

114-115 LONGEST STANDING
RECORDS
Legendary feats from years ago!

116-119 FIGHTING GAMES
Plucky players who pack a punch!

120-125 RECORDS ROUND-UP
An info-blast packed with unbelievable speedruns

126-127 GLOSSARY
Record-setting and speedrunning terms explained

50

60

86
94
116
62
68
90
42
96
114

EVO 2017
LOSERS FINAL
2
1
GGP | KAZ

GO FOR THE HIGH SCORE!

What's the biggest *Minecraft* build ever? How many points is it possible to score in *Pac-Man*? Who are the fastest gamers out there? What are the strangest gaming records? And which are the best games for would-be record breakers to play? We've got all that covered, and much more—prepare to be amazed!

We've got mind-blowing facts and figures from all over the world of gaming—high scores and completion times that are practically impossible to beat, one-off events and world firsts that can never be replicated, and unique records that ingenious gamers have claimed for themselves. All your favorite gaming stars are here, too, from Mario and his record-breaking number of games sold, to DanTDM and his unmatched *Minecraft* empire on YouTube. There's also plenty of expert advice on how to grow your skills, improve your performance, and maybe even go on to set records of your own. Just imagine . . . one day, it could be *your* epic feats of gaming skill featured in a book like this!

THE BIGGEST GAMES EVER!

★ ★ ★

WITH MILLIONS OF COPIES SOLD TO FANS ALL OVER THE WORLD, THESE ARE THE MOST POPULAR AND SUCCESSFUL VIDEO GAMES ON THE PLANET!

MARIO

528 million

First game:
Mario Bros. (1983)
Best-selling game:
Super Mario Bros. (1985) 40m
Most recent game:
Super Mario Odyssey (2017)

Nintendo's mascot has always been a pioneer in both 2-D and 3-D gaming. *Super Mario 64* was a landmark release at launch in 1996, and its perfect 3-D platforming is still almost unmatched over 20 years later. It's also the most popular speedrun game ever—according to the number of recorded runs on **speedrun.com**, three of the top six are *Mario* games.

With over half a billion copies sold across all mainline titles and spin-offs, it's no surprise that there are tons of records across

the *Mario* series. It has given us gaming's longest-serving voice actor—Charles Martinet has been the voice of Mario since 1995. *Super Mario 64* also has the honor of being the only game to have been a launch title for two different generations of consoles—its original N64 release was followed by a port for the DS launch nearly a decade later. Mario himself also holds the record for being gaming's most prolific character in a single year, having appeared in nine games back in 2007 alone. Nintendo's superstar has been *extremely* busy over the years!

Did You Know?

Not counting spin-offs, *Mario* platform games alone have sold over 300 million copies!

MARIO'S BLOCKBUSTERS

How the platform hero's biggest games stack up, by games sold

• SUPER MARIO BROS. (NES, 1985)	40.2M	• SUPER MARIO WORLD (SNES, 1991)	20.6M
• MARIO KART WII (WII, 2008)	35.6M	• SUPER MARIO LAND (GAME BOY, 1989)	18.1M
• NEW SUPER MARIO BROS. (DS, 2006)	29.8M	• SUPER MARIO BROS. 3 (NES, 1990)	17.3M
• NEW SUPER MARIO BROS. WII (WII, 2009)	28.4M	• MARIO KART 7 (3DS, 2011)	13.6M
• MARIO KART DS (DS, 2005)	23.2M	• SUPER MARIO 64 (N64, 1996)	11.9M

TETRIS

495 million

First game:
Tetris (1984)
Best-selling game:
Tetris (mobile) (2008) 425m
Most recent game:
Puyo Puyo Tetris (2017)

Many people think this Russian classic is the perfect video game. It's so simple yet so satisfying, and every well-planned Tetris (the act of clearing four lines at once with a single block) feels like a win. Don't let that simplicity fool you, though. The franchise has also given us what may well be the world's hardest puzzle game! Arcade release *Tetris The Grand Master 3: Terror-Instinct* gets so hard that blocks can drop instantly and even turn invisible towards the end of a run. Only six players are known to have ever achieved Grand Master rank in this game!

Did You Know?

The original Game Boy *Tetris* release was the handheld's best-selling game, with around 35 million units shipped in total!

POKÉMON

290 million

First game:
Pokémon Red/Blue/Green (1996)
Best-selling game:
Pokémon Red/Blue/Green (1996) 31m
Most recent game:
Pokémon Ultra Sun/Moon (2017)

As a true multimedia phenomenon, *Pokémon*'s long list of records expands well beyond gaming. It has the longest-running gaming anime tie-in with over 1,000 episodes in total, as well as the record for tie-in movies with a whopping 20! No gaming series can beat it in the trading card field either, with over 75 sets released in English featuring almost 9,000 unique cards! Back on the gaming side, it's the RPG with the highest number of unique recruitable characters, with over 800 in the latest games. There are also some interesting records within the Pokémon world itself. Cosmoem is a curious example—weighing in at 2,204.4lb (999.9kg), it is the heaviest Pokémon while also being the smallest, a tiny 4 inches (10cm) tall!

WII

202 million

First game:
Wii Sports (2006)
Best-selling game:
Wii Sports (2006) 83m
Most recent game:
Wii Sports Club (2014)

The Wii spawned a whole line of games named after the console, starting with launch title, *Wii Sports*. The sequel, *Wii Sports Resort*, greatly improved accuracy by being the first game to support the Motion Plus add-on for greater control precision, while *Wii Fit* capitalized on the machine's huge install base to turn it into a home fitness tool. These games showcased the power and potential of motion controls, making this arguably the series with the greatest influence over its generation—it led the way for Microsoft's Kinect add-on and Sony's Move controllers.

THE SIMS

First game:
The Sims (2000)
Best-selling game:
The Sims (2000) 16m
Most recent game:
The Sims 4 (2015)

200 million

This life sim started as a spin-off from the popular *SimCity* series. It pulled the camera in closer to let players manage the day-to-day lives of the city's residents. The series quickly found a lot of fans—players have lived dream lives, landed the perfect jobs, and built their ideal homes in the games. There's seemingly no limit to the kind of stories it can tell. While not the first game to feature its own original language (that's 1990 fantasy RPG *Ultima VI* and its gargoyle language, Gargish), it does boast the first major music video recorded in a fictional game language—Lily Allen recorded a version of "Smile" in Simlish!

Did You Know?

EA had modest expectations for the first game. It did a little better than the predicted 200,000 copies, though, shifting an incredible 16 million in total!

FIFA

200 million

First game:
FIFA International Soccer (1993)
Best-selling game:
FIFA 17 (2016) 17m
Most recent game:
FIFA 18 (2017)

While it might not be the longest-running annual sports game (that's *Madden*), EA's *FIFA* series is easily the most successful. It has evolved massively since its creation—the isometric pitch and generic sprite players of the original have been replaced with the ultimate digital recreation of the game day experience.

It's a transformation that began a long time ago too. Even as early as the PS1 games, EA was using actual broadcast commentators and real-world players and teams to give the most authentic soccer experience possible. Sometimes EA has been known to take this realism too far, though—*FIFA 2001* had a scratch-and-sniff disc that let players actually smell the pitch!

SONIC

150 million

First game:
Sonic the Hedgehog (1991)
Best-selling game:
Sonic the Hedgehog (1991) 15m
Most recent game:
Sonic Forces (2017)

Sega's famous mascot has plenty of records to his name, from having the best-selling series on Sega hardware to having the longest-running video game comic tie-in. The games are perfect for speedrunning—aside from a few tricks and glitches, it's all about fluid movement and using the optimal route through each level. The fact that most Sonic games can be completed makes them ideal for people new to speedrunning. Not only are entire runs quite short, but you can also use level select codes in order to practice individual stages as much as you need to!

NEED FOR SPEED

150 million

First game:
The Need for Speed (1994)
Best-selling game:
Need for Speed: Most Wanted, (2005) 16m
Most recent game:
Need for Speed: Payback (2017)

Ever since its 1994 debut, EA's flagship racing series has delivered quality arcade-style racing in some of the world's most exotic cars. Vehicle modification is a staple part of the series, letting players create their own perfect ride. The series doesn't have a huge presence on the speedrun scene, but it doesn't really need it—all of the modern releases have in-game leaderboards, so the majority of competition happens online. EA has also had developers push the series outside of street racing—*ProStreet* moved into circuit racing and *The Run* was a pan-American road trip.

Need for Speed has been through no less than 11 different developers, with games for more than 25 different systems. That's a lot of cars!

LEGO

144 million

First game:
LEGO Island (1997)
Best-selling game:
LEGO Star Wars: The Complete Saga (2007) 15m
Most recent game:
LEGO Marvel Super Heroes 2 (2017)

Video games based on the popular LEGO construction sets have been around for 20 years, but it wasn't until 2005 that they hit the big leagues. Combining LEGO with another franchise (such as *Star Wars*) was a stroke of genius, attracting fans from both franchises. This laid out a perfect template that could be (and has been!) applied to any other series. Warner Bros. is now taking this concept even further with LEGO *Dimensions*. In this crossover adventure, all of your favorite heroes and villains from comics, movies, games, and TV unite!

Did You Know?

LEGO *Marvel's Avengers* has the most playable characters in any LEGO game, with a huge total of 257 to be unlocked or purchased!

FINAL FANTASY

130 million

First game:
Final Fantasy (1987)
Best-selling game:
Final Fantasy VII (1997) 10m
Most recent game:
Final Fantasy XII: The Zodiac Age (2017)

With 15 mainline games behind it, *Final Fantasy* is the second biggest RPG franchise on the planet. On top of those core games, there are spin-off games in so many different genres that it's hard to know where to begin. The strategy battles of *Final Fantasy Tactics*; the *Mario Kart*-like craziness of *Chocobo Racing*; the super cute musical adventures of *Theatrhythm: Final Fantasy* . . . not only is the main series just back-to-back winners, but most of the spin-off titles are also awesome fun.

MADDEN

First game:
John Madden Football (1988)
Best-selling game:
Madden NFL 07, (2006) 10m
Most recent game:
Madden NFL 18 (2017)

144 million

Another EA Sports game makes it onto the best-sellers list! Just as *FIFA* is for soccer, *Madden* is the leading name in football video games. It's so accurate that actual NFL players have been known to use the game as a training aid, while TV broadcasts have even started to use *Madden*-style camera angles for their coverage of real matches. It's EA's longest-running official sports game, now in its 30th year and as strong as ever. While EA's golf, hockey, basketball, and tennis games might not be quite so frequent or popular these days, *FIFA* and *Madden* are here to stay—neither has missed a single year since they first launched.

FIRST DOWN!
RUN BY #35
FOR 3 YARDS

MINECRAFT

First game:
Minecraft (2011)
Best-selling game:
Minecraft (2011) 122m
Most recent game:
Minecraft: Switch Edition (2017)

122 million

It's incredible that such a recent game is able to hold its own among some of the biggest series ever. *Minecraft* is by far the most successful new franchise, already earning it a place in gaming history, spawning spin-offs like *Minecraft: Story Mode*, successful merchandise lines, and much more. Not since *Pokémon* has the world seen such a multimedia phenomenon. The freedom of *Minecraft* makes it a great game for would-be record breakers as there's so much you can do and so many different ways to do it all. Get creative, then get out there and show the world what *you* can do!

THE LEGEND OF ZELDA

89 million

First game:
The Legend of Zelda (1986)
Best-selling game:
The Legend of Zelda:
Ocarina of Time (1998) 12m
Most recent game:
The Legend of Zelda: Breath
of the Wild (2017)

Link has had adventures on every single Nintendo console (apart from the short-lived Virtual Boy) and they're always awesome. It's a series that makes great use of the hardware it's on—the NES original managed to create a fully explorable world on 8-bit hardware, *Ocarina of Time* took the series into 3-D in style, while *Breath of the Wild* delivered a gigantic open Hyrule that takes hundreds of hours to explore. These games are favorites among speedrunners, with thousands of players battling it out for the top times. This constant competition means that these runs are as entertaining to watch as the games are to play!

Did You Know?

Many stars have been *Pro Evo* cover stars, but it's Lionel Messi and Cristiano Ronaldo who have featured on the most—a total of three times each.

PRO EVOLUTION SOCCER

87 million

First game:
Goal Storm (1996)
Best-selling game:
Pro Evolution
Soccer 6 (2006) 4m
Most recent game:
Pro Evolution
Soccer 2018 (2017)

FIFA and *Pro Evolution Soccer (PES)* have repeatedly traded the title of "Best Soccer Game" over the years but today, they fill two quite different gaps. While *FIFA* excels in recreating the match day experience and authentically emulating a broadcast match, *PES* arguably has the edge in terms of gameplay and is better as a video game based on soccer. What it lacks in licenses and likenesses (it does still have a fair few), it makes up in on-pitch variety and sheer depth. Experts can set up perfect dribbles, curve rocketing shots into the top corner, and dance around defenders in all kinds of inventive and skillful ways. *PES* will always be the game of choice for any soccer connoisseurs out there.

GRAN TURISMO

77 million

First game:
Gran Turismo (1997)
Best-selling game:
Gran Turismo 3 (2001) 15m
Most recent game:
Gran Turismo Sport (2017)

Billed as "the real driving simulator," *Gran Turismo* was one of the first console racers to leave arcade-style handling behind. Instead, it relied on realistic physics and fully customizable vehicles, things that have only grown more impressive and complex as the series has gone on. It's by far Sony's most successful exclusive series, outselling its closest rivals by more than 2:1. The series is also known for its incredible vehicle counts—PS3 release *Gran Turismo 6* featured over 1,200 unique cars!

DRAGON QUEST

70 million

First game:
Dragon Warrior (1986)
Best-selling game:
Dragon Quest VIII: Journey of the Cursed King (2004) 6m
Most recent game:
Dragon Quest Heroes II (2017)

This was *Final Fantasy*'s main rival for years until the developers of the two series—Square and Enix—merged in 2003, making them sister franchises rather than competing ones. *Dragon Quest* is hugely popular in Japan, but has struggled to replicate that success outside its home country. Global sales look to be improving recently, however, perhaps because it continues to offer classic turn-based RPG gameplay while its main competitors have shifted towards more action-oriented combat.

RUNNERS-UP

The franchises that didn't quite make the cut

- HALO (65M)
- THE OREGON TRAIL (65M)
- WWE 2K (60M)
- JUST DANCE (59M)
- DONKEY KONG (56M)
- CRASH BANDICOOT (50M)

PAC-MAN

This iconic arcade franchise is one of the biggest and most popular games on the score-chasing scene. In fact, the original release has been played so competitively that it's impossible for anyone to take the best score any higher! That doesn't mean that there aren't thousands of other *Pac-Man* records fans can still fight over, though—with countless versions of the game and lots of modes, you're sure to be able to find a ghost-chomping maze game to call your own!

Pac-Man is the best selling arcade machine, with more than

400,000

sold to date.

There have been

65

official *Pac-Man* games and spin-offs, covering almost every system imaginable!

BEST TIME
02:00.00

X6

Namco and *The Gadget Show* (UK) teamed up to create the largest game ever played projected onto the side of a building—a modified version of *Pac-Man* that was a gigantic

23,881 ft^2 (2,218.65 m^2)!

A perfect game of *Pac-Man* reaches

3,333,360

points, eating all four ghosts with every Power Pill all the way to the "kill screen."

255
The final fully playable level in arcade *Pac-Man*, due to a bug in the game's code.

PLATFORMERS

You could argue that platform games are responsible for games as we know and love them today. Born in the early 1980s, platformers made the most of the technical limitations of the time, tasking players with running and jumping over objects to achieve goals.

But—as with any video game—that challenge was not enough for some players, so many decided to start trying to beat the games super quickly. Enter the speedrun, a trend that would soon spread into other gaming genres as well.

Platformers have come a long way from their humble 2-D origins. While there are still a lot of pixel-perfect 2-D games being developed today, 3-D platformers are extremely popular, too.

It might look cute, but *Ori and the Blind Forest* is actually really difficult!

🏆 THE BIGGEST NUMBERS!

CRASHING THE PARTY

Sony got developer Naughty Dog to make them their own mascot for PlayStation: **Crash Bandicoot**. Crash's games went on to sell over **50 million** copies worldwide, and became one of the most successful American game series in Japan, too.

GOTTA SELL FAST!

For the longest time, **Sonic** was Mario's main rival in the platforming field. Thanks to being on the popular Sega consoles, Sonic managed to shift over **350 million** games to date, although that figure also includes mobile downloads.

IT'S-A ME!

After appearing in *Donkey Kong* (under the name "Jumpman") in 1981, **Mario** went on to become one of gaming's most famous icons. He has appeared in over 200 games, earning franchise sales of over **570 million**!

MARIO MAKER MADNESS

Ever wanted to design your own game levels? Well now you can! *Super Mario Maker* is a game that lets players make their own Mario courses . . . and it's been a huge success! So far, more than **7.2 million** courses have been created and they've been played over **600 million** times, too.

THE HIGHEST VIDEO GAME SCORE EVER

On June 19, 2008, Tom Duncan sat down to play *Garfield*—a simple Atari 2600 platform game from 1984 that was never actually released. Duncan achieved the highest game score ever: **23 quintillion— 23,418,862,404, 272,676,864**, to be more precise!

JIM DAVIS

TOOLS OF THE TRADE

A subset of the speedrunning scene is the "Tool Assisted Speedrun," or TAS for short. This is where players create and use tools that allow for perfect gameplay, enabling feats not usually possible with even the best human reflexes. Speedrun sites tend to track TAS runs and regular runs separately, on account of TAS advantages such as these . . .

SLOW MOTION

When tools first emerged, it was common for them to slow a game down to 5 percent of its original speed, allowing players to improve their timing in any given game.

FRAME-BY-FRAME ADVANCE

As emulators became more advanced, toolers learned how to advance games frame by frame, meaning super-precise jumps and dodges became possible.

MEMORY WATCH

This can be used to see what a game is doing "under the hood" whenever you perform a certain action. That code can then be manipulated for bugs and exploits.

SAVE STATES

Think of this as a game save snapshot that you can simply reload whenever you like, trial-and-error-ing until the desired outcome is reached.

INCREDIBLE FEATS!

PLATFORM PERFECTION

GOOD THINGS IN SMALL PACKAGES

The original *Super Mario Bros.* has a file size of only 256 kilobits—that's **roughly 32 kilobytes**, which is ridiculously small. Some of the images on this page are three times the size of that when stored digitally. You could fit roughly 1 million copies of the original *Super Mario Bros.* on a modern 32GB smartphone!

THE RAREST IN THE WORLD?

In 1991, Nintendo went on a tour in the USA with a game called *Nintendo Campus Challenge*. It was a national tournament where players tried for high scores on short versions of three games—*Super Mario Bros.*, *Pin Bot*, and *Dr. Mario*. After the challenge, all versions of the game (except one!) were destroyed. After being found at a garage sale in New York, the game eventually ended up selling on eBay in 2010 for $20,100.

MARATHON PLANET!

A more recent platform game, *LittleBigPlanet 2*, attracted a lot of very keen players. Sony set up an environment in which players could marathon the game, hoping for a world record and as it happens, David Dino, Lauren Guiliano, and Sean Crowley teamed up to achieve it, racking up a massive **50 hours** on the game.

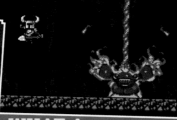

BUILT-IN CHALLENGE

Crash Bandicoot: Warped—the third game in the series—introduced time trials. The developers not only gave players Platinum, Gold, Silver, and Bronze trials to achieve, but they also added in **secret "developer times,"** too. If you beat those, you were better at the game than the dev team!

WHAT A KNIGHTMARE!

Shovel Knight captured gamers' imaginations when it launched in 2014. An interesting retro-styled platformer, it instantly attracted a big speedrunning audience. The quickest Any% run stands at **42m 54s** while the trickier 100% record is currently 1h 03m 08s. Both records were set by Swedish runner Smaugy.

ARE WE OUT OF THE WOODS YET?

Ori and the Blind Forest is a gorgeous platformer with inventive jumping mechanics and a wonderful story, too. To date, the quickest completion of the game sits at **22m 34s** by Swiss player Ikewolf, who also holds the quickest 100% completion of the game at **1h 08m 47s.**

CASH IT IN!

On October 10, 2015, Jamie "Kinnijup" White managed to collect **$3,404,400** in *Spelunky*, narrowly beating previous record-holder twigglefly's impressive $3,399,600. The **5.5 hour run** can be watched online, and even blows away the creator of the game—Derek Yu—who thought a score of $3,000,000 would be impossible to achieve.

MEAT'S BACK ON THE MENU!

Widely regarded as one of the toughest platformers ever made, Team Meat's *Super Meat Boy* is the Holy Grail of speedrun achievements. The Any% category of the game changes hands regularly, but on January 8, 2017, Hamb managed to complete the game in **17m 41s**—just 2s quicker than previous record-holder, Vorpal.

HARDEST MARIO MAKER LEVELS

P-BREAK
Wii U—2015
COURSE ID
6059-0000-005E-4FB5

1 You know it's a hard *Mario Maker* level when its completion percentage is super low. It's a badge of pride for any *Mario Maker* player to have beaten this. Better yet, it's a level that's only really possible to play in *Mario Maker* thanks to the game's unique ability to let Mario wear a Buzzy Beetle shell as a helmet. There have been 7 million attempts at the level, but only just over 1,000 clears to date—creator PangaeaPanga isn't exactly known for making Mario's life easy!

MY LITTLE KAIZO: SPIN IS MAGIC
Wii U—2015
COURSE ID AC93-0000-0121-A1D8

2 This is a hellish vision of a *Mario Maker* level. The majority of it relies on you grabbing a Bob-omb early on and carrying it with you as you progress. Timing the throws, catches, and bounces on the bomb through a constant, perilous 50-second journey is *really* tough. There's only one clear way through the level, thanks to how it's been designed. Do you have what it takes to tame this beast of a stage?

FAIL'S FLOTILLA: FINAL FLIGHT
Wii U—2017
COURSE ID
154E-0000-0358-C2FB

3 The most recent creation on this list, and arguably the hardest of them all. It took creator Failstream over 400 hours just to clear his own level *once* in order to upload it! Since then, it's only been beaten by one other player—16-year-old Flipside managed to show off his mastery of the cape to beat the level after "just" 72 hours of trying! The stage is all about taking out obstructions without ever losing the cape, before making one epic glide to freedom.

Did You Know?

If you played every level in *Super Mario Maker* for one minute each, it would take you over 14 years to play them all!

OR YOU COULD TRY . . .

N++

If you don't have access to a Wii U or 3DS to play *Super Mario Maker*, don't worry—there are similar games out there that let you test yourself against levels other people have made. *N++* is a game that has its own pre-built levels for you to practice in, and an editor to take on super-tough custom ones, too. There are thousands to attempt!

LITERALLY, LONGEST MAP POSSIBLE

Wii U—2015
COURSE ID
DA8E-0000-002A-DC4D

5 *Super Mario Maker* has limitations on the number of blocks you can place in a single level. This creator managed to use this to their advantage to work a level around on itself seven times, creating the longest possible route. So, it's not hard, just tedious. There are no enemies, no hazards, no switches—just an endurance test. Be careful at the very end of the level, though!

KAIZOTASTIC 3

Wii U/3DS—2015
COURSE ID E1A7-0000-00F0-BD3A

4 This is a level that requires perfect timing and a lot of determination to see it through to the end. It's sitting on a clear percentage of less than one percent and over 30,000 players have tried this out around the world. The main tactic here is to toss shells and springs in mid-air and bounce off them to perform double-jumps of sorts around all those spikes. All that while the level scrolls on and the entire floor is lava? Craziness!

MARIO VS. SONIC

Sonic was created as an alternative to Mario. The family-friendly plumber was all bright colors and iconic sounds; Sonic was designed to be cooler—to have style. It took a while for him to speed up, but by Sonic's second game, he and Mario were battling it out to be the most popular mascot in video games!

Competition like this improves the games and is exciting to be a part of as players. To honor this great gaming rivalry, we've put together some of the craziest Mario and Sonic achievements. Whatever the numbers say, we think they're both awesome!

SONIC THE HEDGEHOG FASTEST COMPLETION
Sonic The Hedgehog
10m 53s
SUPER MARIO BROS. FASTEST COMPLETION
Super Mario Bros.
4m 56s

The quickest speedruns for both entries in the series are from the first games—they were the smallest titles in each franchise. *Sonic* takes longer because there is a lot of game to get through, whereas *Super Mario Bros.* has a few tricks you can use to skip entire levels, primarily the warp pipes.

SONIC THE HEDGEHOG: MOST EXPENSIVE GAME
$981.33
Sonic the Hedgehog
MARIO: MOST EXPENSIVE GAME
$20,100
Nintendo Campus Challenge

We covered the Mario Campus game on page 22, but the Sonic cartridge has a good story, too: a version of the game for Master System appeared in Europe, but dressed with a US barcode and sticker. This was enough of a rarity to coax collectors into a mad bidding war, ending at just under $1,000.

SONIC THE HEDGEHOG: HIGHEST SCORE
3,261,260
Sonic the Hedgehog 2
MARIO: HIGHEST SCORE
2,272,840
Super Mario Bros.

Eric Schafer of the US is responsible for the incredible score in *Sonic the Hedgehog 2*—a feat that can only be achieved by absolutely rushing through the game but taking time to collect as many rings as possible. Score chasing in *Sonic* is hard, but Schafer made it look like a breeze.

RAREST AMIIBO
Sonic Amiibo
$30
Princess Peach Amiibo
$25,100

Defective Amiibo sell for a premium to collectors thanks to their unique nature. Toys that are made incorrectly at the factory can end up making crazy profits for people that happen to find them in stores. One such Amiibo, a legless Princess Peach, sold for an incredible $25,100 on eBay in 2014.

SONIC THE HEDGEHOG
Total Appearances
92
MARIO
Total Appearances
211

Another win for Mario, and by a long way. Nintendo's mascot has proven that he's capable of more or less anything, from karting to competing in the Olympics. While Sonic has seen his fair share of cameos and crossover appearances, he just can't quite keep up with gaming's most famous star . . .

SONIC THE HEDGEHOG
Collected Cast of Characters
31
MARIO
Collected Cast of Characters
30

This is a hard one to judge, because both series have a lot of crossover characters. We've chosen only characters that were introduced or are integral to the universe of the series in question—for Mario, for example, we've not included *Donkey Kong* or *Wario*-universe characters. It's close!

8 TOP TIPS

HOW TO BREAK RECORDS

PLATFORMING MADE SIMPLE

START WITH SOMETHING EASY

1 To become a pro, start somewhere easy. Go for a game that has no known glitches, has very few random elements to deal with, and—ideally—is quite easy and short.

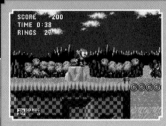

MASTER THE MECHANICS

2 Platformers have a few very important mechanics. Jumping is the most important, so any game you play, learn how the jump works—know exactly how far you can get, as well as how high you can get. Don't take risks at first. Know your limits.

READ PIXELS

3 A common term in platform speedrunning is "pixel perfect." This relates to jumps or tricks that require perfect accuracy to perform, such as jumping off a ledge at the last possible moment. Learning to read and judge such distances is a crucial skill to work on!

LEARN HOW TO DEAL WITH RNG

4 A lot of games can be predicted—you can run through the whole game the same way multiple times with nothing changing. But some games have randomized enemies or features. Learn how the randomness (or RNG) of dangerous zones works and figure out the best way to safely deal with hazards.

WATCH THE PROS

5 If you're struggling to get past a certain area or shave significant chunks of time off your record attempts, go online and look at channels like Games Done Quick or even just YouTube replays of previous record runs. These might show tactics you hadn't seen before, or even just inspire you to play more and try harder!

LOOK INTO TOOL-ASSISTED SPEEDRUNS

6 Tool-assisted runs could make it a lot easier for a new speedrunner to get their feet on the ground (no pun intended): they make tricky jumps, impossible shots, and incredible feats doable. While setting up a TAS can be hard, just watching tool-assisted runs online can reveal helpful tricks, skips, and time saves.

INVESTIGATE GLITCHES

7 The vast majority of speedruns exploit glitches to make the time you can complete the title in quicker and more attainable. It's not cheating: in fact, there's a healthy community of players that make a point of discovering glitches and learning how best to manipulate them. See what you can find!

MAKE TIME FOR IT

8 No one ever became a master at speedrunning on their first venture into the field; you're going to need to attack the same game, the same levels, the same bits of levels, for hours and hours at a time until you're good enough to go for a record. But practice makes perfect—speedrunning requires perfection.

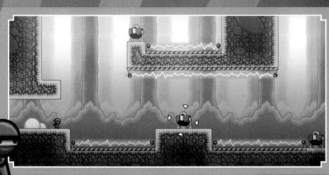

TRAINING GAMES

LIMBO
A simple 2-D game that can be easily learned and has few mechanics in the way that could slow you down.

SUPER MEAT BOY
Super Meat Boy's short levels, easy mechanics, and brutal difficulty curve will really put you through your paces.

SUPER MARIO BROS.
There are a bunch of exploits to learn: this is a great place for getting used to glitches.

CRASH BANDICOOT: WARPED
Warped offers in-game targets, with some really tough, no-tools challenges built-in.

ROLE-PLAYING

★ A CLASS OF THEIR OWN

RPGs have been popular as long as video games have been a thing: there's something about an experience that wraps you up in its world that manages to capture the imaginations of many different types of gamer.

These games are so big that there are usually many different ways to complete them. This offers a unique challenge to speedrunners and record-breakers because it makes them want to find the quickest path through the game.

Since RPGs rely heavily on numbers and calculations, they allow players to really dissect and take advantage of bugs—in some cases, you can smash through a game in a fraction of the time the developers intended if you know how to exploit the right things. And that's just what some of our record holders here have managed to do . . .

Did You Know?

2014 RPG *Child of Light* was written to incorporate poetry throughout—every single sentence in the game rhymes!

THE BIGGEST NUMBERS!

WHAT A BUDGET

Final Fantasy VII goes down in the record books as being the game with the biggest budget of any JRPG ever made. The production of the game itself cost a massive $45 million and promotion cost $100 million (in 1997)!

GOTTA SELL 'EM ALL!

The most popular RPGs ever made were the original *Pokémon* games: *Red*, *Green*, and *Blue*. They're all considered one game, so collectively these three games sold over 23,000,000 copies worldwide.

WHEN WORLDS COLLIDE

Kingdom Hearts is a crossover RPG series which merges Disney with *Final Fantasy*. The concept might sound odd, but it has proved to be hugely popular—it's the best-selling crossover RPG series with over 22.2 million units sold across the series.

IT'S OVER A TRILLION!

Japanese PS Vita game *Trillion: God of Destruction* has an interesting gimmick. The final boss has 1,000,000,000,000 HP and you know that from the beginning. It's even in the title! That's the highest HP count ever for a boss in a single-player game.

IT'S ABOUT TIME

Most RPGs take a lot of our time to finish—some can run into hundreds of hours—but that's nothing compared to what the characters in *Chrono Trigger* go through. During the course of the game, the timeline stretches across 65,000,000 years—comfortably the longest time period spanned in any RPG.

TWITCH PLAYS POKÉMON

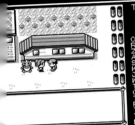

"Twitch Plays *Pokémon*" was a social experiment that had players from all around the world simultaneously try to play through the original *Pokémon* game by inputting commands into the Twitch chat feed. It was chaotic, silly, and a lot of fun, and the crazy phenomenon achieved . . .

1.1 million players

36 MILLION VIEWS | 122 million commands issued

16 DAYS | 7 HOURS 45 minutes & 30 seconds runtime

121,000 PEAK PLAYERS

INCREDIBLE FEATS!

MEET THE VERY BEST, LIKE NO ONE EVER WAS . . .

THE FIRST ACTION-RPG?

Action-RPGs are now more popular than turn-based ones, but that wasn't always the case. 2-D action-RPG *Dragon Slayer* hit PCs in 1984 and the genre was born—it had combat emphasis, limited inventory, and exploration: all things that'd come into the genre later on. Without this, we wouldn't have the variety of games we do today!

THAT'S SOME SUPPORT

UnReal World was originally released in 1992, but that doesn't mean the game is forgotten. It's actually still quite popular, and holds the record for being the longest supported game of all time—there have been updates from its creators for 25 years! That's not bad going for a game developed by just two people . . .

TIME FLIES . . .

Not all speedruns are what you might consider fast. In fact, a 100% run of GameCube RPG *Baten Kaitos: Eternal Wings and the Lost Ocean* takes more than **two solid weeks**! French runner Baffan currently holds this crazy record, with a total time of 341h 20m 03s.

OLDER THAN YOU THINK

Final Fantasy might get all the attention for being one of the most famous JRPG series, but it wasn't the first. It was actually preceded by *Dragon Quest*, a game series that began in 1986—a whole year before the first *Final Fantasy* game came out. *Dragon Quest* is still going strong today, too, although it's primary fan base is in Japan.

TOO MANY FRIENDS!

1995 PlayStation game *Suikoden* holds the record for having the most recruitable characters in an traditional RPG. There are **108 characters** that you can convince to join your army. Some are trickily hidden, and others aren't even used in battle. This record may be beaten by a *Fire Emblem* game soon, though!

ARE YOU BLIND?

In August 2015, US gamer Shenanigans managed to clear the whole of *Pokémon Blue* while blindfolded! The speedrunner learned all the glitches he needed to know to get through the game and then matched all the audio cues necessary to trigger them. He also learned a few basic step routines and set the record live at Summer Games Done Quick in front of a worldwide audience.

FANTASIES DON'T HAVE TO BE FINAL

Despite running for 15 games, *Final Fantasy* isn't actually the most prolific RPG series out there. Bandai Namco's *Tales* series just edges out *Final Fantasy*—as of 2016's *Tales of Berseria*, there are **16 mainline entries** in the popular RPG franchise.

A NEW HERO RISES

Tactical RPG series *Fire Emblem* has always been a celebrated part of Nintendo's roster and in 2017, the publisher released the **first mobile version of the game, *Fire Emblem Heroes***. People were unsure if the tactical RPG would find success on mobile, but on the first day of release, it made **nearly $3 million!**

TOP FIVE POKÉMON

WORLD RECORDS

POKÉMON RED/ BLUE CLEAR, NO SAVE CORRUPTION
GameBoy, 1996
RECORD 13:30—pokeguy84
DATE SET October 30, 2016

1 This involves five steps. First, the game is started as normal, choosing the starter Pokémon and beating the rival. Next, they have to catch a Pidgey as quickly as possible. Then, an Escape Rope item glitch is used to bypass the Brock battle and walk through most of the game, entering the Cerulean Cave and catching Ditto. This can then be used to glitch the game, leading to a simple walk through to the end of the Elite Four to win!

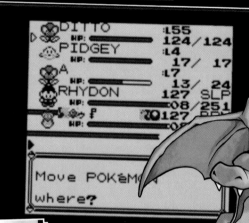

Pokémon Red/Blue Any% No Save Corruption 807		
Rival	+22.4	2:54
Pidgey	-10.3	6:37
Brock Skip	-3.7	9:15
Ditto	-10.4	11:18
Done		13:54
		12:56.60
PB: 2:25.90		
Best: 1:59.93		1:38.42
Possible Time Save		25.97
Best Possible Time		13:18

Pokémon Diamond/Pearl Any%		260
Rival	-1.2	20:51
Roark	-7.3	24:51
Mars	-1:16	35:41
Gardenia	-1:10	47:32
Jupiter	-1:21	54:07
End		1:00:12
		55:54.33
Previous Segment		-10.5
Possible Time Save		0.00

POKÉMON GOLD/ SILVER, GLITCHES
GameBoy Color, 2000
RECORD 16:34—Consair
RECORD SET April 25, 2017

3 This run looks pretty standard to begin with, but things quickly take a strange turn. Once you're out of the intro stage of the game, you can simply enter a Pokémon Center and start uploading and downloading Pokémon using the PC. The trick? Giving Pokémon certain strings of characters for names actually tricks the game into reading the wrong code . . . then you move through the world seemingly at random until the credits roll!

POKÉMON DIAMOND/ PEARL CLEAR, GLITCHES
Nintendo DS, 2006
RECORD 58:49—crafted
DATE SET February 2, 2017

2 The main exploit in this run is using the DS's internal clock to trick the game into thinking certain times or events have passed when they haven't. The record holder in this run managed to figure out a way to minimize wild Pokémon appearances by manipulating RNG—by walking only on specific tiles, most encounters can be avoided. Thanks to this, it's now a really fast run.

Did You Know?

There are 4,294,976,296 different variations of the Pokémon Spinda, because its markings are determined by the unique stats of each individual monster.

ONE TO WATCH

Keisuke

?!

POKÉMON SUN/MOON, ANY%

3DS, 2016
RECORD 5:13:13—itotaka1031
RECORD SET January 1, 2017

4 You might notice that this run is much longer than the others. That's because there haven't really been any bugs found in the 3DS's newest *Pokémon* entries yet, and players simply have to blast through the game as quickly as possible in order to complete it using all the vanilla tools available. Glitches, tricks, and skips will probably be found eventually to help bring that time down but for now, anyone looking to challenge this record has a long adventure ahead of them!

DIGIMON STORY CYBER SLEUTH: HACKER'S MEMORY

The newest *Digimon* title is a sequel to the popular *Cyber Sleuth* game that came out on PS4 and Vita in 2016. *Digimon* games work similarly to *Pokémon*, but tend to have more RPG elements. *Hacker's Memory* has over 300 Digimon to recruit and fight with, too— perfect for people who have caught every Pokémon!

POKÉMON RED/BLUE— CATCH 'EM ALL

GameBoy, 1996
RECORD 1:47:59—Stringflow
RECORD SET February 19, 2017

5 The Catch 'Em All run uses a glitch in the game's core code to skip through various in-game locations and manipulate RNG to spawn each kind of Pokémon on command. This version of the run takes you up to Brock, where you skip the gym, and then straight to the Power Plant to catch some of the rarest Pokémon as early on as possible. You then work your way back from there, filling the Pokédex as you go.

★ STEP INTO A WORLD OF FANTASY

Final Fantasy is one of the most famous brands in gaming, so naturally the games are among the most hotly contested RPGs in terms of records. While a casual playthrough of a *Final Fantasy* game can take anything up to 100 hours, keen adventurers are always finding new tricks to cut hours from runs. It's impressive to see these epic games beaten so quickly, but it's even cooler to do it yourself. Watch and learn as the pros play, then see if you can match their speedy heroics!

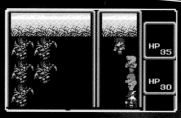

FINAL FANTASY
NES, 1987
Sales: 2.5 million
Fastest Speedrun: 7m 09s—Luzbelheim
Fun Fact: The game is called *Final Fantasy* because director Hironobu Sakaguchi thought it could be his last game—he was ready to give up on games if it didn't sell well.

FINAL FANTASY II
NES, 1988
Sales: 1.7 million
Fastest Speedrun: 2h 35m 49s—nickynoel
Fun Fact: Confusingly, the SNES game that was released as *Final Fantasy II* in the US was actually *Final Fantasy IV*—the NES versions of II and III only released in Japan, leading to some strange sequencing!

FINAL FANTASY III
NES, 1990
Sales: 3.8 million
Fastest Speedrun: 6m 21s—Luzbelheim
Fun Fact: Completing the game in such a short time involves using a major glitch to skip right to the credits. The best times without using this trick are just under an hour, which is still amazing!

FINAL FANTASY IV
SNES, 1991
Sales: 4.5 million
Fastest Speedrun: 1h 56m 01s—the_roth
Fun Fact: The main speedrun tactic in *Final Fantasy IV* is using something called the "64-door hierarchy glitch," which forces the game into thinking one door acts as another. This lets you skip large chunks of the game.

FINAL FANTASY V
SNES, 1992
Sales: 3.1 million
Fastest Speedrun: 3h 48m 07s—swed7
Fun Fact: The Chemist job is particularly useful to speedrunners. It offers potions that temporarily boost your party's levels, which can save a lot of grinding!

> Galuf: Can we get into Exdeath's castle?
> Zeza: Sure. We have everything perfectly planned out!

FINAL FANTASY VII
PlayStation, 1997
Sales: 12 million

Fastest Speedrun: 7h 34m 46s—Luzbelheim

Fun Fact: *Final Fantasy VII* is one of the most popular PlayStation games ever, but it wasn't originally planned for Sony's system. Early tests were done for the N64, but it was discovered that the cartridge-based console wouldn't be able to cope with such a massive game.

FINAL FANTASY VI
SNES, 1994
Sales: 4 million

Fastest Speedrun: 50m 37s—TheSabin

Fun Fact: Don't bother trying to cure or inflict the Blind ailment. Due to a bug in the game's code, this "negative" status effect doesn't actually do anything!

FINAL FANTASY VIII
PlayStation, 1999
Sales: 8.9 million

Fastest Speedrun: 7h 20m 42s—jester1610

Fun Fact: Many speedruns of *Final Fantasy VIII* use a memory card-like peripheral (called the PocketStation) and a mini-game called *Chocobo World* to harvest items and make the route through the game quicker and easier.

FINAL FANTASY IX
PlayStation, 2000
Sales: 5.7 million

Fastest Speedrun: 8h 49m 34s—Luzbelheim

Fun Fact: Many players believe that *Final Fantasy I* and *Final Fantasy IX* are set in the same world—the world maps across both titles are remarkably similar, as are some of the games' aesthetics.

FINAL FANTASY X
PlayStation 2, 2001
Sales: 15 million

Fastest Speedrun: 10h 16m 05s—CaracarnVi

Fun Fact: Despite being the first fully-voiced game in the series, hero Tidus' name is never spoken as it can be changed by the player. If you're wondering though, it's pronounced "tee-dus!"

FINAL FANTASY XIII
360, PS3, 2009
Sales: 7.6 million

Fastest Speedrun: 4h 54m 36s—LewdDolphin21

Fun Fact: *Final Fantasy XIII's* supporting character Vanille was originally cited as being the main character of the game, but when some promotional art released with Lightning as the focus, the development team had to change their minds.

FINAL FANTASY XII
PlayStation 2, 2006
Sales: 5.2 million

Fastest Speedrun: 5h 52m 46s—roostalol

Fun Fact: A remake of *FFXII* came out in 2017, and included rebalanced enemies, new jobs, new modes, and an overhauled graphics engine.

FINAL FANTASY XV
PS4, Xbox One, 2016
Sales: 6 million

Fastest Speedrun: 4h 53m 56s—TheOOT

Fun Fact: *Final Fantasy XV* was in development for over ten years, and when it finally released it became the best-selling RPG on both the Xbox One and PS4 overnight.

8 TOP TIPS

HOW TO
BREAK
RECORDS

LEVEL UP YOUR RPG SKILLS!

GET A BASELINE

1 RPGs are usually very long, so if you want to speedrun one, you're going to want to know how much time you'll need to put aside. Figure out where you can save time, use save stats, make backups, and learn the game inside out on your first run through.

BREAK IT DOWN

2 Because RPGs are such massive projects to tackle, you're going to want to break down every element of your run into easy-to-digest bits; think about every menu operation you'll use, every glitch, every tactic, every trick. Learn every one inside out, but not during a run: just get to know them.

SPREAD IT OUT

3 When you've got all the mechanical bits down, start splitting the game up into chunks—make frequent saves during your first playthrough. That way, you can return to any section to practice individual parts without having to replay the entire game, which is extremely helpful.

TEST RUN

4 Once you've got the mechanics, the cues, the game, and the tactics down, try a full run. Expect things to go wrong the first few times. Note down split times from the sections you split the game down into, then compare those to a world record run. Knowing where you need to improve is a key part of this.

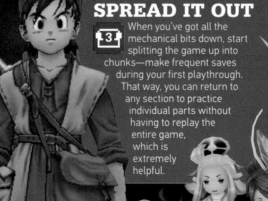

RESIST THE RESET

5 When you're practicing with RPGs, it's easy to just restart and try the whole thing again if something goes wrong. You'll quickly tire yourself out if you do this, though. Try to persevere, even if you know you can do better next time: you won't improve as much overall if you just play the opening section over and over again.

RECORD EVERY ATTEMPT

6 Even if you're having a practice go at a record, make sure you record it. If you manage to do something incredible, it's always going to be better if you have it on record—that way, it can always be verified, or shared for research purposes.

USE THE COMMUNITY

7 The speedrunning community is one of the nicest collectives on Earth. If you're struggling with a section or a trick, check out sites like speedrun.com and you'll find the best runners, handy video guides, and advanced routes and techniques, all in one place!

DON'T BE AFRAID OF TOOLS

8 Once you're able to get through full runs consistently, have a look at some tool-assisted runs of the same game. Even as a practice tool, this can help you think in frames rather than seconds, and it'll generally help you play to a higher standard.

TRAINING GAMES

SUPER MARIO RPG
A game that will always have an audience when you stream, *Super Mario RPG* is an entry-level RPG that'll break you in.

FINAL FANTASY VII
With a massive following behind it, and a huge legacy, *FFVII* is an essential speedrunning experience.

KINGDOM HEARTS
Develops skills across various disciplines, including action combat, platforming, item usage, and menu navigation.

FIRE EMBLEM: AWAKENING
This is a wonderful game to practice dealing with RNG on—luck plays a huge part.

RPGS How to Break Records

ALL-TIME GAMING RECORDS **39**

HALL OF FAME

DONKEY KONG

No game's high score has been more hotly contested than *Donkey Kong*, Nintendo's classic 1981 arcade game. As with *Pac-Man*, the existence of a "kill screen" (here caused by a glitch that causes players to start Level 22 without enough time to finish the stage) means scores can only get so high, which really helps drive competition. DK himself has gone on to become a huge star for Nintendo in his own right, too, and it all started right here!

The *Donkey Kong* high score world record has only changed hands **16 times** in the 36 years since it was first set!

1,218,000 Current *Donkey Kong* high score record, set by Wes Copeland back in 2016.

32:19 Fastest time to complete SNES platformer *Donkey Kong Country.*

ACHIEVEMENTS & TROPHIES

★ UNLOCKING THE BEST

As well as competing for high scores in single games, players today can fight over high scores **across** *all* **games.** Achievement systems track progress for every game played, and your Gamerscore or Trophy Level is an indicator of just how committed you are to gaming greatness. It's not just the total that matters, either—getting 1,000G in a super-tough game, or a Platinum Trophy that just 0.1 per cent of players have is massively satisfying. These systems really encourage friendly competition, so let's take a look at some of the current leaders . . .

Did You Know?

Avatar: The Last Airbender—The Burning Earth has the easiest Achievement list ever. You can get all 1,000G in about a minute!

🏆 THE BIGGEST NUMBERS!

LIMIT BREAK

Microsoft has rules about the values developers can assign Achievements. On top of the usual 1,000G cap for a full game, a single Achievement can only go as high as **500G**. Only two games actually go that high—*Brave: A Warrior's Tale* and *2006 FIFA World Cup*.

A NEVER-ENDING COMBO?

To unlock the Never Ending Combo Achievement/Trophy in DrinkBox Studio's *Guacamelee!*, you have to perform a combo of **over 200 hits** with the main character Juan—that's the longest chain in any side-scrolling beat-'em-up game in the world!

HOW MANY TROPHIES!?

Sony has announced that over **25 billion Trophies** in total have been unlocked across the PlayStation 3, PlayStation 4, and PS Vita since 2008. That means, on average, players have unlocked almost **3 billion** Trophies per year since the service went live.

GOING FULL STEAM!

Valve's PC gaming platform Steam was ahead of Sony in putting achievements onto its service. And when it arrived, it arrived in style: there are currently over **270,000 achievements** you can earn on Steam, and over **9,500 games** support the reward system, with players from **252 countries** registered as having unlocked at least one.

WHAT AN ACHIEVEMENT!

Xbox players have nabbed over **500 million** individual Achievements over the lifespan of both Xbox One and Xbox 360, according to Exophase. That's around **125,000** Achievements earned for each of the 4,000+ tracked Xbox games on average!

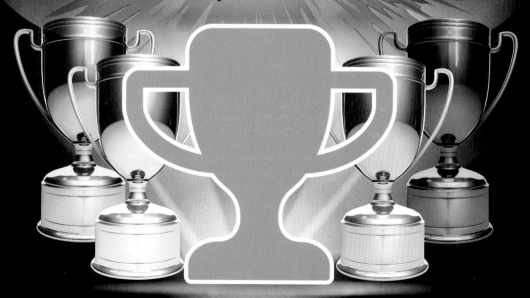

These are the worst **0G** Achievements you can earn on Xbox Live!

NBA Ballers: Chosen One
Loser
Lose 5 Ranked Matches in a row

Dirt Rally
Mondays Be Like ...
Crash your car so badly it ends the race

Oddworld: New 'n' Tasty
Oops
Accidentally destroy a fellow Mudokon

FIFA 08
Beat Yourself
Score two own goals in a single game

The Simpsons Game
Pwnd
Injure yourself ten times in a row

Guitar Hero III
Tail Between Your Legs
Turn down a challenge from a Rock God

Superman Returns
Not That Super
You got caught cheating . . .

🏆 INCREDIBLE FEATS!

MASTERS OF UNLOCKING

> Most *Halo* speedruns are done on either Easy (quickest) or Legendary (most impressive).

SAY HALO, WAVE GOODBYE

Halo 5 is one of the biggest Xbox One exclusives, but its Achievement data tells us that not many people actually saw it through to the end. Only 27% of players have the Achievement for finishing every mission on Normal difficulty, dropping to 8% and 3.5% for Heroic and Legendary respectively. That means well over three million owners haven't even completed the game!

POETRY IN MOTION

When top Steam Achievement hunter Xeinok wanted to unlock a reward in *Frozen Synapse* years after it released on PC, he needed to beat one of the game's developers. Xeinok got creative and sent them a personal poem, requesting an in-game duel. **"I had to play the game of my life!"** Xeinok said—it must have been the most stressful gaming session of all time!

THE FUNNY THING IS . . .

Most games use Achievements and Trophies to tempt players into performing tasks that they otherwise wouldn't really bother with. Some have a little fun with the reward system instead. There are games like *Portal 2* that use **achievements as extra jokes**, and other games, like *The Stanley Parable*, just use them to make players question their motivations.

TIME CONSUMER

Some rewards take longer to unlock than others—notable Trophy hunter crisding89 stated that he'd spent **1,000 hours** on *White Knight Chronicles* trying to unlock the game's Platinum: that's over **41 full days** of playing the game, using the same character to achieve it all. Now *that's* commitment.

THE FIRST EVER ACHIEVEMENTS

The first ever achievement was not for the Xbox 360, the PS3, or the PC. In fact, **it debuted in 1982**, thanks to Activision. The publisher set out high scores to beat for each of its games and by taking photographs of the TV screen after breaking the set score and sending them to Activision, players could earn iron-on patches for their trouble!

HOW LONG!?

One of *Rayman Legends'* rewards requires players to "reach the final level of Awesomeness." This requires you to beat other players in time trials . . . but in order to unlock the Achievement, you have to post great times in every task the game sets you for six solid months!

Up to 1,000G is available per Xbox game, with a few exceptions—*Rare Replay* offers 10,000G!

SOMETHING FOR THE WEEKEND

The most famous Xbox Achievement chaser is **Stallion83**— a celebrity in the Achievement world thanks to his insistence on chasing down rewards. His busiest period as an Achievement hunter was just before the launch of the Xbox One. He played over 50 games and unlocked over **17,000 Gamerscore** over the course of a weekend!

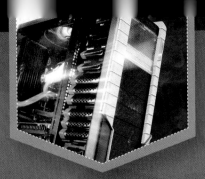

THE RAREST STEAM ACHIEVEMENTS

Steam makes it extremely easy to track and compare achievements with friends, so it's always great to add a rare reward to your virtual trophy cabinet. Here are a few of the trickiest ones to unlock, if you're feeling brave . . .

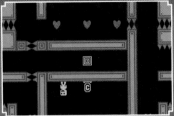

VVVVVV
MASTER OF THE UNIVERSE
COMPLETE THE GAME IN NO DEATH MODE
Game Owners: 1,100,000
% Unlocked: 0.4%
Much like *Super Meat Boy*, this retro-style platformer is *really* hard. Only 1% of players have managed to finish it within 50 lives, so it's hardly surprising that only a handful of experts are able to beat the game with a single life!

THE STANLEY PARABLE
GO OUTSIDE
DON'T PLAY THE STANLEY PARABLE FOR FIVE YEARS
Game Owners: 2,100,000
% Unlocked: 0%
The Stanley Parable's achievement list is playful and clever, but this reward is one of the craziest we've seen. The game released in October 2013, so this will be impossible to get until late 2018 at the very earliest!

CRUSADER KINGS II
NOT SO BAD
SURVIVE THE END TIMES
Game Owners: 1,400,000
% Unlocked: 0.1%
A very tough strategy game, *Crusader Kings II* has a variety of achievements sitting at 0.1% despite having a pretty large player base. This achievement will pop if you manage to survive a plague. You have to make sure you have hospitals and prisons to get through something like this.

TRAIN SIMULATOR
DLC ACHIEVEMENTS
Game Owners: 1,000,000
% Unlocked: 0%
It's not that *Train Simulator* has impossible achievements, nor is it that people find the game boring or don't want to play the scenarios to get the rewards. No, instead, thanks to *Train Simulator*'s DLC adding up to $6,254, it simply means many players can't afford the DLC in the first place in order to get the achievements!

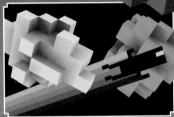

BIT.TRIP BEAT
MEAT.BOY SMELLS
GET A PERFECT IN WORLD 1-1 USING A GAMEPAD
Game Owners: 311,000
% Unlocked: 1.6%
Many PC gamers much prefer using a mouse and keyboard to a controller. In *Bit.Trip Beat*, it gives you a greater degree of accuracy too, so playing with a pad is effectively playing on hard mode. You can't miss a single beat, and there are *loads* to hit!

GARRY'S MOD
ADDICT
SPEND ONE YEAR PLAYING GARRY'S MOD
Game Owners: 13,200,000
% Unlocked: 1.8%
Garry's Mod requires you to put a crazy amount of time into unlocking one achievement—this isn't asking that you play the game for a bit once a day for a year . . . no, it wants 8,760 hours. It's an actively tracked stat, so you need to be in-game for it to count.

THE 🏆 RAREST ACHIEVEMENTS

Microsoft's Xbox 360 was the first console to offer an Achievements system, and fans have been enjoying the race towards ever-higher Gamerscores since. These are some Achievements that only the most dedicated players will have unlocked . . .

 PINBALL FX2
PERFECTIONIST **[200G]**
0.01% Complete the Sorcerer's Lair table in one game

 NEED FOR SPEED
GOLD PLATED **[80G]**
0.01% Win Gold on all Prestige events

 TETRIS ULTIMATE
TETRIS MASTER **[125G]**
0.01% Earn Show-Off, T-Spinner, and Simply the Best badges

 GIANA SISTERS: TWISTED DREAMS
DIRECTOR'S CUT—HARDERCORE **[200G]**
0.01% Unlock Uber Hardcore mode

 RARE REPLAY
STAMPERS FOREVER **[150G]**
0.01% Get every stamp in the game

 ELITE: DANGEROUS
TRIPLE ELITE **[150G]**
0.02% Rank Elite in Exploration, Combat, and Trading

 GIANA SISTERS: TWISTED DREAMS
DIRECTOR'S CUT—BRILLIANT! **[200G]**
0.02% Get Five Stars in all Hard mode levels

 PINBALL FX2
OBSIDIAN OBSESSION **[200G]**
0.04% Collect 13 obsidians on Sorcerer's Lair table

THE MOST ELUSIVE PLATINUMS

PlayStation Trophies attract a certain kind of obsessive hunter to them. Sony platforms have Platinums. They are badges of honor, and the following represent some of the rarest on PS4 . . .

 STARDEW VALLEY
0.01% PS4

 STREET FIGHTER V
0.01% PS4

 MIGHTY NO. 9
0.01% PS3, PS4

 GUITAR HERO LIVE
0.01% PS3, PS4

 SUPER MEAT BOY
0.01% PS3, PS4, Vita

 LITTLEBIG PLANET3
0.01% PS3, PS4

 TITAN SOULS
0.01% PS3, PS4, Vita

 SKULLGIRLS ENCORE
0.01% PS3, PS4, Vita

 OLLIOLLI2: WELCOME TO OLLIWOOD
0.01% PS3, PS4

 GEOMETRY WARS 3: DIMENSIONS
0.01% PS3, PS4, Vita

 NBA 2K14
0.03% PS4

🏆 THE MOST COMMON PS4 PLATINUMS

- ROCKETS ROCKETS ROCKETS **86.11%** of players
- THE INNER WORLD **86.16%** of players
- ORC SLAYER **86.36%** of players
- GEM SMASHERS **86.45%** of players
- TESLAGRAD **86.46%** of players
- MONSTER JAM: CRUSH IT! **87.36%** of players
- HER MAJESTY'S SPIFFING **88.78%** of players
- JAZZPUNK **90.64%** of players
- ENERGY CYCLE **96.23%** of players
- THE WORLD OF NUBLA **98.33%** of players

THE GREATEST TROPHY & ACHIEVEMENT HUNTERS OF ALL TIME

Each platform has its own hero—the player that has managed to smash records and get established as the most decorated PlayStation and Xbox gamer in the world. We caught up with both platforms' heroes to discuss what drives them to be the very best.

XBOX
PLAYER: STALLION83
GAMERSCORE: 1,632,034
CLAIM TO FAME: Gamerscore leader for 11 years, first player to break 1 million Gamerscore

Need a Gamerscore boost in seconds? Give Avatar: The Burning Earth a try!

How did you first get into collecting Achievements?
Getting into Achievements came very naturally to me. I've always enjoyed playing tons of different games and genres. That mentality just carried over when the Xbox 360 launched and the Achievements started to click with me pretty early on, then after the Achievements started to click, I had the urge to increase my Gamerscore. And the rest is history.

Did you start with games you enjoyed or did you just play pretty much anything?
I go through cycles. I'll play just about anything but if I don't feel like playing games just for the Gamerscore, I'll play the games I enjoy more and not really focus on my overall Gamerscore, but focus on the Achievements in a specific game that I really like.

How do you feel about Trophies—do they interest you as much?
Achievements are better than the copycat Trophies because they came along first, but I'm glad PlayStation has their own system. I wish Nintendo would follow suit.

Does this take up a lot of time?
I would be lying if I said this doesn't eat up the majority of my time. It's gotten easier over the years because the selection of games has gotten larger with ID@Xbox games but being the first to the one million Gamerscore mark and doing it in the time frame I did it in, that absolutely took up so much time. I had to sacrifice a lot in my life to reach that goal.

Do you find gamers in the industry respect you for your success?
I feel like there's a fair amount of respect given when it comes to what I have accomplished with Achievements and Gamerscore. I don't expect many people to truly understand what it took because if you haven't done it like I have, how would you know what it takes to achieve such a thing? There are several gamers that try to get under my skin but I've been dealing with that for over a decade and I'm just numb to that type of dialog.

What's been the stand-out moment of your Achievement-hunting career?
There are two stand out moments during my Achievement-hunting career: when I was the first person in the world to break one million Gamerscore on March 13, 2014, and the other is being awarded the only Lifetime Xbox Live Gold membership card. Major Nelson presented that to me during the Xbox One launch in New York. Man, that was beyond awesome. I was on cloud nine.

What advice would you offer to younger players looking to earn as many Achievements as possible themselves?
ID@Xbox games is the source of easier Gamerscore nowadays. I didn't have the luxury of those easier games during my run up to a million Gamerscore and yes, I'm pretty jelly that people get to have an easier path to the bar I set with a million Gamerscore. Another great way to get games is using the Xbox Live Game Pass service. That gives you access to 100+ games for a low monthly fee. That's a lot of potential Gamerscore.

CATCHING UP . . .
smrnov: 1,628,755G
Celtic Force: 1,474,865G
RedmptionDenied: 1,297,943G

PLAYSTATION

PLAYER: HAKOOM
TROPHIES: 60,000 (1,326 PLATINUM TROPHIES)
CLAIM TO FAME: First player to reach Trophy Level 100, most Platinum Trophies

> Hakoom was playing PS3 games before Trophies were added!

How did you first get into collecting Trophies?
Back in 2008, Sony said they would release a patch that awards gamers with Trophies. I got interested and waited until it got released. It was very rewarding when the Trophy popped on the screen and it just felt good when earning it.

Did you start with games you enjoyed or did you just play pretty much anything?
I started playing the PlayStation back in 2006. I used to play nearly every single game released even if it wasn't good. There were no Trophies back then, though. After the Trophy system was released, I started playing games I had never even heard of just to earn the Trophies! It's like collecting something like baseball cards, or stamps, or whatever hobby a collector has: once you pop, you can't stop!

How do you feel about Achievements—do they interest you as much?
I feel that the Achievements on Xbox are lacking value, because they are just plain numbers and don't mean anything. Like, for example, if you compare to Trophies, there's Bronze, Silver, Gold, and *then* you earn a Platinum when you get 100 per cent. Achievements on the other hand are just numbers: numbers until you have 1,000 . . . which is still just a number! So I have no interest regarding that because the value is just weak in comparison.

Does this take up a lot of time?
Yes, it takes a lot of my time, if not all my time! Back in my prime days, I used to play nearly all day because I had no job or responsibility. Now, I have a job, and a wife, and a kid, so the time has become less, although I still play a lot. Even at work, I take my Vita and sometimes my PS4 to play. But as you see, I still earn a lot of Trophies even when I have less time; the reason for that is because every year, there are more games and more Trophies that only take a few hours or even minutes to obtain.

Do you find gamers in the industry respect you for your notoriety?
Back in the day, it was a 50/50 balance: some respected me and some didn't. But now, it's the opposite. Many gamers respect me now and also interact and speak with me everyday, but the number of negative interactions has dropped from 50 percent to maybe only 10 percent.

Is there a good community of Trophy hunters?
Yes, there are many communities, but the best communities I found are from PSNTL and PS3imports. They're very friendly and helpful when I compare them to other communities, which are often filled with trolls.

What advice would you offer to younger players looking to earn as many Trophies as possible themselves?
My advice would be to stay away from Trophies and Achievements and just play the games you enjoy. Following the path I or any other Trophy hunter did will only lead you to fall into a loop of playing games you don't enjoy and getting your temper up every single time over something not worth it!

CATCHING UP . . .

Roughdawg4: 1,321 Platinums
nmxwzy: 1,248 Platinums
xLukk: 1,151 Platinums

MINECRAFT

When a game is as popular and open-ended as *Minecraft,* there's plenty of record-breaking potential. From finishing the game in under five minutes to earning every achievement in the game, amassing lots of mobs in the same place to lightning-fast crafting . . . every aspect of the game can be contested—and bested— by avid adventurers.

You won't believe just how fast the best players can finish the game. And maybe some of the crazy things people have done will inspire you to go out and set some records of your own— and we've got some handy hints on doing just that!

Did You Know?

Minecraft's popularity has meant it has outsold entire franchises already, including huge games like *FIFA* and *Madden!*

🏆 THE BIGGEST NUMBERS!

A RECORD-BREAKING INVESTMENT

In 2014, Microsoft acquired *Minecraft* developer Mojang for an incredible **$2.5 billion**. This is the highest price ever paid for a non-mobile-exclusive game studio, and the third highest price paid for *any* game studio, behind Activision's purchase of *Candy Crush* developer King (**$5.9 billion**) and Tencent picking up *Clash Of Clans* developer Supercell (**$8.6 billion**).

TOP OF THE WORLD (ALMOST)

Minecraft is the second-best-selling game of all time, with over **120 million copies** sold to date. Out in front is *Tetris*, the classic puzzle game that had a 27-year headstart. In fact, if you take that time into account, then the tables are turned, with around **17.5 million sales** per year on average for *Minecraft*, compared to **14.5 million** for *Tetris*. Mojang reported in 2016 that it was selling a whopping **53,000 copies** every day!

SO MANY MINERS!

According to data from Mojang, *Minecraft* has more than **55 million monthly players**. To put that number into context a little, that's a monthly player base somewhere between the total populations of South Africa and Italy. The *Minecraft* team pointed out that a conga line comprising this many people would stretch all the way around Earth!

MINECRAFT MANIA

YouTube is packed with awesome *Minecraft* videos, but it's DanTDM that has the world's most popular *Minecraft* channel. He was recognized by Guinness World Records in August 2016 with an incredible **7.9 billion views** across his videos, and that number has since soared past the **10 billion** mark!

AN ENTIRE COUNTRY!?

The largest *Minecraft* map to date was built by the Danish government back in 2014. It's a **1:1 scale map** of Denmark created for educational purposes, made from around **4 trillion individual blocks** over about **16,600 square miles** (43,000km^2) of virtual space. Although it's fairly simple in terms of design, it still weighs in at a **massive 1TB**!

SETHBLING

A quick glance at his YouTube channel is all it takes to realize that Seth is a real-life *Minecraft* master builder. Seth helped pioneer the discovery of some of the techniques used in high-level speedruns, and his all-round skill in *Minecraft* is exceptional. Not only has he proven this with amazing survival runs, but he's also gone on to build some of the most incredible things we've ever seen. The most impressive of these is a fully working Atari 2600 emulator that plays multiple games, and while it's really slow, the mere fact that it plays games like *Donkey Kong* and *Space Invaders* alone makes it an incredible feat of virtual engineering! Check out his channel if you're ever short of inspiration—you might even get some ideas for new records and runs you could attempt yourself!

⊞ INCREDIBLE FEATS!

FASTEST COMPLETIONS

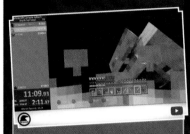

ANY% SET SEED

This category starts from a new save file and is all about reaching and defeating the Ender Dragon as quickly as possible, using whatever tricks and glitches you like. A fixed seed of the player's choice is used, allowing for a game world that is the same every time and so can be learned.

 **16:14
(BRAVEN, 2017)**
Using the seed "-561453290158161019", BraveN spawns extremely close to a village that has both a chest containing tons of useful supplies, and several villagers who can trade many Emeralds thanks to a glitch. There's also an End Portal underground nearby, allowing for an extremely speedy completion.

 **4:07
(JOSHGAMING4, 2015)**
Even though PC runs don't include loading times (this run clocked in at 6:37 in real time), it's still *much* faster than the console runs due to using save and world state manipulation to duplicate items. The seed used was "882658115306501881", spawning right into a village and leaving the Nether with a second portal that leads right to an End Portal.

ANY% SET SEED GLITCHLESS

All glitches are banned in this category, so it just comes down to the fastest possible legitimate completion of the game. Again, fixed seeds are used, allowing players to figure out where all the best resources are before going for world record time on maps where everything needed is within easy reach.

 **32:06
(BRAVEN, 2017)**
This run used the same seed as BraveN's quicker glitch-assisted time. Getting all the required materials naturally takes a little longer without being able to trick villagers out of Emeralds, but it's a great run all the same!

 **7:32
(THEESIZZLER, 2017)**
"-2063810908146531904" is a seed that sets players up perfectly for crazy speedruns, and this one is amazing to watch. From cleverly using a small lava pool to engineer a Nether Portal early to beating the Ender Dragon with snowballs and exploding beds, this run does in mere minutes what many players haven't been able to achieve in *years* of play!

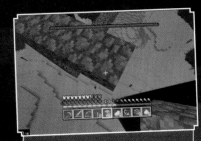

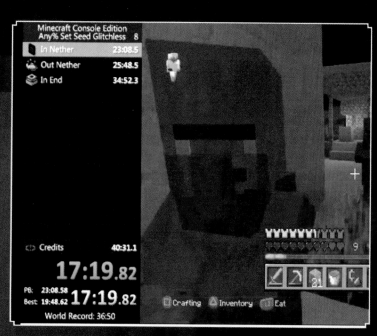

ANY% RANDOM SEED

Unlike using a fixed seed, there's no amount of planning that can speed runs up in this category—resource placement is all left up to chance, so everything comes down to player adaptability, knowledge, and skill. It's a less popular category than Set Seed, since there are just too many variables at play to make it truly competitive.

 1:03:13
(ROBTHEGAMER115, 2017)

This was achieved on the Xbox 360 version, as it has smaller worlds than the others, so the best chance of having things you need nearby. Even so, the struggle to find lava slowed this run down—there's room for improvement through better seed luck, so people are sure to keep trying to beat it.

 9:52
(ILLUMINA1337, 2015)

As with the glitched Set Seed runs, use of save state manipulation makes the PC record significantly faster than the console one. The runner reset the game hundreds of times before finding a seed that was speed-friendly, and the nearby temple and village set up the rest of the run perfectly.

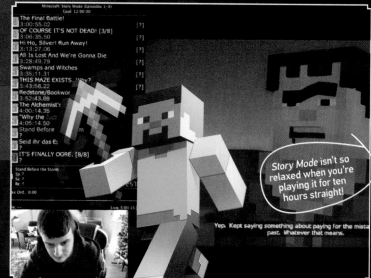

MINECRAFT: STORY MODE (ANY%)

9:25:10
(JHOLLEWORTH, 2017)
He openly admits that the run didn't go as smoothly as he'd like, but this record-holder isn't likely to get an awful lot of competition on this time as few people want to sit down and play straight through all eight episodes in a row! The run—particularly toward the tail end—is surprisingly smooth, but there's only so much time-saving you can do in a story-based game like this . . .

CRAZY CHALLENGES!

A TOWN BUILT FROM SCRATCH
(CHARLEY DUNCAN, 2015)
40 HOUSES
built in three in-game days

ONE SWITCH TO RULE THEM ALL
(TEXASHOKIES, 2015)
12,360 DOORS
opened using a single lever

SNOW MESSING WITH THIS RECORD . . .
(GILBERTO QUINTERO, 2016)
65 SNOWMEN
built in one minute

THE BUSIEST BAKER IN MINECRAFT
(MARIO_12323, 2017)
181 CAKES
crafted in five minutes

Did You Know?

There's so much you can do in *Minecraft* that setting your own records is easy—just choose something nobody has done before and record yourself doing it!

A HOLE LOT OF ZOMBIES!
(DEADMOUSE BOSS, 2017)
4,391 ZOMBIES
crammed into a 1x1 hole

WORLD SIZES

Before the Better Together update, *Minecraft's* procedural worlds came in many shapes and sizes. Check out how big (and small!) these are in comparison to one another . . .

Did You Know?

Players with the Better Together update are able to play with one another in infinite worlds, regardless of what system they are on!

PC

POCKET (CURRENT)

PS4/XB1 LARGE

PS4/XB1 MEDIUM

PS4/XB1 SMALL

360/PS3/WII U/VITA

59,999,968×59,999,968×256
(921,599,016,980,802,562,144 blocks/m3)

16,777,216×16,777,216×256
(72,057,594,037,927,936 blocks/m3)

5120×5120×256
(6,710,886,400 blocks/m3)

3072×3072×256
(2,415,919,104 blocks/m3)

1024×1024×256
(268,435,456 blocks/m3)

862×862×256
(190,219,264 blocks/m3)

POCKET (ORIGINAL):
256×256×256
(16,777,216 blocks/m3)

* not to scale

SELLING POWER

In early 2017, Microsoft announced that *Minecraft* had sold over 121 million copies across all platforms since launch. Breaking down those numbers, it gets even more impressive . . .

121,000,000
copies sold total in 63 months means, on average:

23,000,000
copies per year

1,920,000
copies per month

443,000
copies per week

63,000
copies per day

2,600
copies per hour

44
copies per minute

So, on average, a copy of *Minecraft* is sold
EVERY 1.33 SECONDS.
Wow!

THE FAR LANDS

In earlier versions of *Minecraft*, there existed a strange place called the Far Lands. Here, the game would corrupt world data and create crazy landscapes the likes of which you'd never normally see. While this has now been patched out, YouTube channel **Far Lands or Bust** is on a mission to reach this place on foot—this adventure will take a while! After **six years and 640 episodes**, Far Lands or Bust is still only a quarter of the way to reaching the Far Lands—at this pace, it'll take **another 18 years** for them to get there!

START POINT

3.1 mln

12.5 mln

FAR LANDS

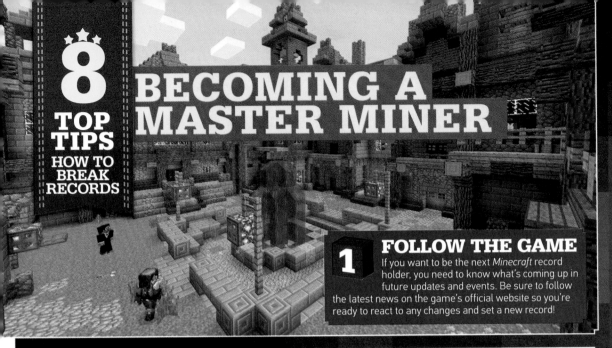

8 TOP TIPS
HOW TO BREAK RECORDS

BECOMING A MASTER MINER

1 FOLLOW THE GAME

If you want to be the next *Minecraft* record holder, you need to know what's coming up in future updates and events. Be sure to follow the latest news on the game's official website so you're ready to react to any changes and set a new record!

2 BE THE FIRST

If you can't be the best, try being first—find a new kind of record to set and you'll have your record, even if someone manages to beat it later. Better yet, do something no one can ever do again—if you were first to beat the Ender Dragon, nobody could ever take that away from you!

3 GET CREATIVE!

The more inventive and personal your newly-created record category is, the more likely you are to hang on to it for longer. Things that take a lot of time or effort are far less likely to be challenged, so go all-in on a project if you want to stay a champion for longer.

4 MULTIPLE VERSIONS

Given the differences between versions of the game on different formats, it could be that you could still be best or fastest on your chosen system, even if the record is higher. By taking a record from the PC version and doing it on console, you're creating a whole new category for yourself.

5 KNOW YOUR LIMITS

Things like high-level speedruns take months, if not years, to master. If you have the time and willpower to commit to going after these impressive records, then great—best of luck! But if not, set your sights a little lower. We can't all be world-class athletes, rockstars, or even gamers, but it's still fun!

6 USE SEEDS

Seeds are handy because you know exactly what you'll find in a world, meaning you can practice things like execution (how you perform the basics of gameplay) rather than worrying about resources. Creative mode can be a similarly useful crutch while trying to improve your skills, too.

7 LEARN FROM THE BEST

Check out some record runners on YouTube to see what the best players are doing, and how they do it. This can teach you how to improve on your basic skills, or it could inspire you to do something you may not have thought of. Inspiration can be found anywhere!

8 WELCOME FEEDBACK

Whether it's friends and family watching you play, or comments on videos, be open to constructive feedback. Working out your weaknesses is the first step to building on them and improving, so don't get mad if somebody points out where you could do better.

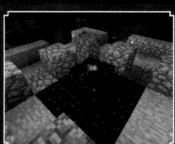

TRAINING GAMES

TERRARIA
Depending on what you're trying to achieve, it might be easier to trial your record in 2-D first before going to 3-D.

DON'T STARVE
If you're looking to set a record in Survival mode, experience with other kinds of survival games will always be helpful.

MIRROR'S EDGE
3-D platforming skills will help you get around faster and more freely, plus you might work out routes you wouldn't have tried.

ROBLOX
There's nothing quite like seeing just how inventive other creators can be. Try a little bit of everything—it's good for you!

PERFECT RUNS
GAMING FEATS THAT CAN NEVER BE TOPPED!

HIGH SCORE
260   260

810286

PAC-MAN
3,333,360

This is the most famous example of a "perfect" high score. The reason it cannot be beaten is simple—after clearing **stage 255**, a memory error corrupts the play area and kills the run. If you've played perfectly to this point, your score will be exactly **3,333,360**. Billy Mitchell was first to perform this back in 1999, but several other players have managed it since. In fact, one player achieved *Pac-Man* perfection in just **3h 42m**!

POKÉMON RED/BLUE
0h0m

While speedrunners used to run an anything goes Any% category, it was retired once it was discovered that you could beat the game in no time at all! Using a glitch called Arbitrary Code Execution, skilled players can manipulate the menus to modify game data and leap straight to the Hall of Fame, with the in-game clock claiming that not even a single minute has passed.

1UP   HIGH SCORE
009200   026100

DONKEY KONG
1,218,000

This one's debatable, as it's theoretically possible for somebody to come along and eke a few more points out of *DK*. It's unlikely—the run is over three hours long and record holder Wes Copeland squeezes all **21 cycles** for as many points as possible. Similar to *Pac-Man*'s infamous killscreen, a memory issue on **stage 22** leaves Jumpman with only seven seconds to clear the level, so nobody will ever get any farther.

THEATRHYTHM FINAL FANTASY: CURTAIN CALL

9,999,999

Hitting every note in any song with a Critical rating (perfect timing) will result in your final score maxing out at all the nines like this. In the original game, players could only get this score via the "Stoic" bonus for using no equipment or items—without it, scores capped out at **7,999,999**. In *Curtain Call*, however, this requirement was removed, so perfect play will always lead to this score.

WII SPORTS BOWLING

300

Just like in real-life bowling, the maximum score that can be achieved in this Wii launch title is a whopping **300**. To achieve this, you need to hit a strike on all **12 frames**—the point bonuses from each will stack on top of one another to boost your score all the way up to this impressive cap. A perfect game is much easier to achieve in *Wii Sports* than in real life, but both are doable with skill and practice!

Did You Know?

darbian's *Super Mario Bros.* run is super close to being perfect—even using tools to create an actual perfect run, the result is only a few frames off what is humanly achievable!

RIVER RAID

!!!!!!

This **Atari 2600** air combat game is coded to finish as soon as your point counter ticks past **999,999**—your plane explodes, your score is replaced with exclamation points, and the game ends. It's actually surprising that Activision accounted for players even getting that far—when the game first came out the developer would reward a "high score" of as low as **15,000** with a special sew-on patch!

THE EDITOR SAYS . . .

LUKE ALBIGÉS, FORMER *GUITAR HERO* WORLD RECORD HOLDER

If you're looking to set perfect scores of your own, music games are the best place to start. By working your way up to the hardest difficulty, you'll be able to learn and master every single pattern. Remember to make use of practice modes to go over tricky sections until you're comfortable with them, and bear in mind that other mechanics may influence a perfect score. In *Guitar Hero*, for instance, you'll also need to smartly plan out Star Power usage so that every activation doubles your score for the most notes possible. Good luck!

SPORTS GAMES

★ **IT'S ALL KICKING OFF!**

I f you're into competition, you can't really go wrong with sports games! Sports gaming has been around almost as long as video games themselves, and ever since soccer players were made out of little pixelated blocks, gamers have been challenging one another to beat the highest scores, win the most competitions, and of course, defeat each other in whatever sport it is that they choose.

Almost every sport has a video-gamer version. Of course there's football, basketball, soccer, and tennis, but there are also games based on diving, darts, and even dodgeball!

Do you have what it takes for the intense pressure of high-level sports gaming?

🏆 THE BIGGEST NUMBERS!

CRAZY SALES!

The biggest-selling sports game in history is the mighty *Wii Sports*, with a whopping **82.81 million sold as of March 2017**. Now, it probably helped that it was packed in with the Wii, but nevertheless, those are crazy numbers.

MOST EXPENSIVE RARE SPORTS GAME

Incredibly, if you want to grab yourself a copy of *Family Fun Fitness Stadium Events*, an ancient NES athletics game, you will need to pay approximately **$21,166**! Crazy money!

TALLEST PLAYER

Ever fancied playing as the tallest sportsman in history? Gheorghe Muresan, an NBA player from the 1990s, is an incredible 7'7" tall and featured in a load of games, like *NBA Live*, *NBA Jam*, and *NBA ShootOut*.

LONGEST RUNNING SPORTS FRANCHISE

With a history going back over 40 years, *RBI Baseball* is the world's longest-running sports-game franchise, with its original version called *Family Stadium* appearing in **Japan in 1986**. And just to prove its power, a new version actually hit consoles just last year. What a home run!

BIGGEST PRIZE IN SPORTS GAMING

Players good enough to win the grand prize in the FIFA Interactive World Cup walk away with an incredible **$200,000, plus a trip to FIFA's annual awards ceremony**! And the runner-up even gets $100,000.

GOING PRO! INCREDIBLE FEATS!

AND THE CROWD GOES WILD!

Sports gaming is becoming so massive that real-life sports teams are actually signing up gamers to play for them! Manchester City, one of the biggest soccer teams in the world, signed Kieran Brown to their roster to compete in *FIFA 17*. Kieran is one of the best FIFA players out there, and Manchester City joins the likes of Paris Saint-Germain, Schalke FC, and West Ham in signing eSports players. Wow!

TONY HAWK PRO SKATER 3
ALL CHALLENGES 8m 15s

For most people, even loading this game up and choosing your character takes at least five minutes, but the amazing FaytetLT smashes every single goal, level, and gold medal in *Tony Hawk's Pro Skater 3* in an incredible eight minutes and 15 seconds. And if you watch the video, he doesn't even sound like he broke a sweat doing it! He mastered the route through every level of the PC version to make sure he didn't miss a single item or trick. Amazing.

MARIO STRIKERS CHARGED
FLAWLESS RUN
2h 12m 10s

This is a difficult game to master, because your opponents can use their supercharged strikes to score up to six goals at a time, meaning matches can be lost in the last second, and there's not much you can do about it. Unless, of course, you're Danzaiver00, who completed a flawless run to the gold cup in just over two hours, meaning he won every single game and barely conceded a goal. A true *Mario* master!

MOST GOALS SCORED WITH GOALKEEPER IN FIFA 17
SCORE 21

Even on the easiest difficulty setting, scoring with your goalkeeper is hard. So, scoring 21 times with your goalkeeper is practically unheard of. That didn't stop Fred Bugmann from attempting this feat through the Twin Galaxies website, and scoring a record 21 goals. Have you even scored that many goals in a *FIFA* match with anyone? Even with a team made entirely out of Ronaldos, scoring once every in-game four minutes is a supreme feat of skill. But with the keeper? Well, that's truly incredible.

MARIO GOLF TOADSTOOL TOUR
FULL COMPLETION
1h 6s 23ms

When you see milliseconds recorded in a time, you can tell that people take completion times very seriously. This is another really tricky one, as there's enough unpredictability to throw off any speedrunner's entire game. All it takes is a strong gust of Mushroom Kingdom wind to blow that ball off course and the entire run comes crashing down faster than a Thwomp in Bowser's castle. This is actually one of the most fiercely competitive sports-game speedruns out there, so Bluekandy can be very proud of his record.

> Mario and Donkey Kong used to be enemies, but now they're golf buddies!

```
          SCORE          WORLD REC
HI       98520       ┌──────────────┐
1P       98520       │    18m08      │
2P                   │              │
                      QUALIFY   13m00
1P     18m08        1st TRY    18m08
                    2nd TRY    14m26
                    3rd TRY
──────────────────────────────────────
SPEED
         ████████████  1089 cm/sec

I

         TRIPLE JUMP        K

      .13   14   .15   16   .7   1

47
```

TRACK AND FIELD
ALL EVENTS COMPLETED 7m 11s

Ah, the classic. This is probably the most competitive sports game of all time. Mastering one event is an achievement, but doing all eight in less than eight minutes is the highest level of track and field possible. Bayrock has a narrow one-second lead over his nearest competitor, but may not hold onto it for long.

HARRY POTTER QUIDDITCH WORLD CUP
COMPLETED WORLD CUP
35m 38s

Is it really a sport? Hogwarts fans would say so, and who are we to argue with them? If you want to hold the record for completing the *Quidditch World Cup* faster than anyone else, then you will have to do it quicker than Lazar181 and his impressive 35 minutes and 38 seconds. Mount your broom!

CRAZY SPORTS GAME RECORDS!

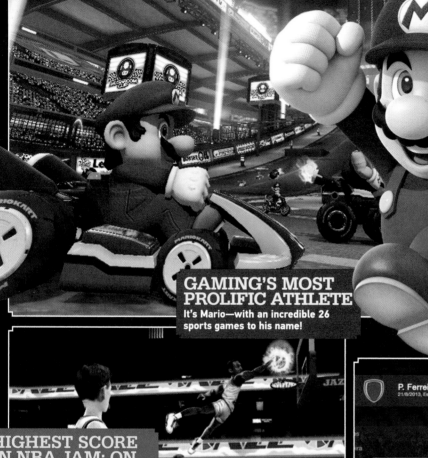

GAMING'S MOST PROLIFIC ATHLETE
It's Mario—with an incredible 26 sports games to his name!

HIGHEST SCORE IN NBA JAM: ON FIRE EDITION
In late 2016, Hal Hawkins managed to score an amazing 151 points in a full match of this Xbox 360 arcade basketball title. He held his AI opponents to just 17 points, winning by a massive margin of 134!

P. Ferreira v A.C. Milan
21/8/2013, Estádio Abel Alves de Figueiredo (European Champions Cup)

MOST PERFECT GAMES OF WII BOWLING IN A ROW
An incredible 20,000, bowled by now retired John S. Bates.

LONGEST EVER GAME OF FOOTBALL MANAGER
Soccer-mad Darren Blanc played for 154 consecutiv seasons on *Football Manager* before he destroyed his game save by spilling liquid on his laptop. His in-game manager would have bee 185 years old!

FIFA INTERACTIVE WORLD CUP

WHAT A PRO-SPORTS GAMING EVENT LOOKS LIKE

Every year, *FIFA* players compete for hundreds of thousands of dollars in the finals of the *FIFA* Interactive World Cup. 32 of the best *FIFA* players from all over the world battle it out for the prize, where their skill and mental strength are tested to the limits. It's always an amazing show!

THE **5** WEIRDEST SPORTS GAMES

1 ROCKET LEAGUE

It has become one of the most popular games in the world, but it's still weird. Soccer. With cars. That can fly. What!?

RIBBIT KING

Golf. With frogs. If you have never played *Ribbit King*, you have never experienced one of the weirdest games in PS2 history.

2 WINDJAMMERS

A new version is now available on PS4, but this Neo-Geo classic is actually a game about competitive Frisbee! It's fast, furious, and seriously fun!

3

4

SPORTS FRIENDS

With four crazy games in one package, including the hilarious BaraBariBall and even funnier Pole Riders, this is a perfect game to play with your buddies.

#IDARB

A crazy combination of soccer, basketball, and platform gaming, with bizarre commentary and even the ability for people to send out Twitter hashtags to change the rules on the fly.

5

8 TOP TIPS

HOW TO BREAK RECORDS

TRAINING TIPS FROM THE PROS

1 PLAY LOTS!

Getting a wide range of sports games is a great way to get to grips with becoming a truly elite player. Most sports games have you controlling an entire team, and those skills are transferable.

2 PICK YOUR SPORT

Once you've leveled up in different sports, it's time to pick your favorite and focus on getting *really* good at it! Are you a soccer fan, maybe you're mad for *Madden*, or do you like to dominate the court in *NBA 2K*?

3 HIT THE TRAINING MODES

Almost every sports game has a dedicated training mode, and they're great for honing your skills—perfect if you're trying to become a world-class player! Be sure to make full use of all the different practice modes your chosen game offers.

4 WATCH THE PROS

Once you've chosen your game and drilled down on your skills, it's time to watch the pros to study how they play. Even just watching the best players in the world can help your game. Learn from the best!

SPORTS GAMES How to Break Records

5 START STREAMING!

It can be daunting to put your gameplay out into the big wide world, however, it's a really great way to learn how to deal with the pressure of an audience, or a high-score, or even a timed run you're looking for. If you find it difficult to do it in front of invisible strangers, then you won't be able to compete at the top levels. You've got nothing to lose, so give it a go, if your parents are OK with it.

7 FIND HIGH-LEVEL OPPONENTS

The best players in the world have high-level "sparring" partners to play against regularly—training partners who push you to play at your best, so you can prepare yourself for competition. Find a friend who's willing to help out here!

6 ENTER TOURNAMENTS

The best way to start truly testing your skills is to enter real-world tournaments. Ask your parents' permission first, but taking on the best players in your area is the best way to judge just how good you are, and what you need to work on.

8 TRAIN YOUR WEAKNESSES

This is a tough one. When you're playing casual games, spend some time focusing on what you're *not* good at. Try a different formation, try new skill moves, try new tactics. You may lose games and get frustrated, but eventually you'll improve in those super important areas!

TRAINING GAMES

FIFA 18
One of the most popular sports games, it gives an understanding of how team-based sports games work.

NBA 2K17
Makes you master precision, tactics, and patience, as well as demanding high levels of skill. It also looks amazing!

TRACK AND FIELD
The best way to destroy your controller, it separates the great players from the ordinary, and focuses on timing and pressure.

ROCKET LEAGUE
One of the only team-based sports games where you only control one "character." Great for pressure, skill, and tactics.

UPER
ARIO 64

Not including digital downloads on Virtual Console, *Super Mario 64* has sold more than **22 million** copies worldwide.

**ch title for the Nintendo
sole and one of the most
ant video games ever**
Super Mario 64 showed how
mes could transition from
3-D. It's a near-perfect
m game—one so loved by
at it's *still* the most popular
un game in the world over
rs after it was first released.
w fast *you* can beat it!

1,607
Number of tracked
Super Mario 64
speedrunners on the
speedrun.com
leaderboards.

39m 28s
kest time to grab
l 120 Stars and
nish the game,
record currently
eld by cheese05.

6m 44s
Fastest time to complete the game, which involves skipping every Power Star!

The original N64 release had **120** stars to collect. The DS port added another 30, for a grand total of **150**.

GAMING TREASURES

FOR THE HOARD!

Certain bits of gaming history are really rare and, therefore, very valuable. And some collectors will pay crazy money to collect these little nuggets of gaming gold.

Whether it's a particularly rare game that had limited copies printed, a special regional variation of a classic, or a new console that turned out to be a dud, there's a lot of video gaming-related treasure out there . . . you just need to know where to look.

We've meticulously combed the archives to find the most valuable gaming treasures out there today. Hang on to your favorite games and consoles—or even those you think aren't very good— they might be worth a fortune one day!

NINTENDO

STADIUM EVENTS

Year: 1986	Platform: NES
Rarity: 9/10	Average cost: $20,000

S tadium Events was published by Bandai in 1987 and was played with the *Family Fun Fitness* mat—a controller you used by walking or jumping on. Eventually, Nintendo bought the rights to sell the mat and promptly pulled and destroyed all copies of *Stadium Events*.

As a result, only an estimated 200 copies of the game exist—and only 20 of those have been accounted for. In 2010, one copy emerged in North Carolina and was sold on eBay for $13,105. Another copy emerged in Kansas later and went for $41,300! The game's box alone has been sold for an incredible $10,000, too.

1990 NINTENDO WORLD CHAMPIONSHIPS [GOLD]

Year: 1990	Platform: NES
Rarity: 9/10	Average cost: $26,000

I n 1990, Nintendo ran a competition across 30 cities looking to find the best NES player *ever*. Players had to achieve high scores in *Super Mario Bros.*, *Rad Racer*, and *Tetris* . . . all in six minutes. The top three finishers received a gray cartridge, making 90 of these in the world. These sell for a lot, but gold versions go for even more.

To earn a gold version of the game, you had to win a promotional contest in *Nintendo Power* magazine. According to Nintendo, only 26 of these gold carts were ever made—which is why when they rarely appear for sale online, they can sell for over $26,000!

EXERTAINMENT MOUNTAIN BIKE RALLY & SPEED RACER COMBO CART

Year: 1995	Platform: SNES
Rarity: 7/10	Average cost: $3,000

L ife Fitness, an exercise equipment company, wanted to capitalize on the success of video games in the early 90s. The company released an exercise bike with a TV screen built-in, along with a special SNES with controls embedded into the bike handles.

Two games were designed specifically for the bike/console: *Mountain Bike Rally* and *Speed Racer*. Because the bike was generally quite expensive, very few copies of the dedicated game ended up selling (since you couldn't play them on a normal SNES). Carts with both games on can fetch $3,700 if they're factory sealed!

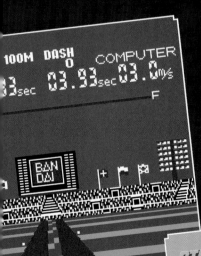

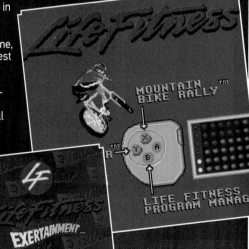

ATARI

ATARI COSMOS

Year: 1981	Platform: N/A
Rarity: 10/10	Average cost: $20,000

The history behind the Atari Cosmos is a pretty sad story: the company was confident in its cutting-edge handheld console, with its LED display and holographic images. But when it publicly exhibited the console at a toy fair in 1981, everyone hated it.

Despite ad campaigns being run and boxes being manufactured, Atari pulled the plug at the last minute: it's estimated five were made overall. Three are empty mock-up units, and two are supposedly fully functional. One exists in the Atari History Museum, and a former employee of the company has the other.

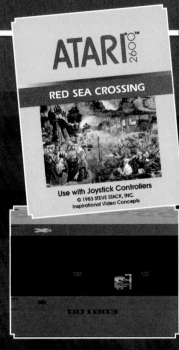

RED SEA CROSSING

Use with Joystick Controllers
© 1983 STEVE STACK, INC.
Inspirational Video Concepts

AIR RAID

Year: 1982	Platform: Atari 2600
Rarity: 9/10	Average cost: $31,000

Aside from being one of the most interesting looking gaming carts of all time (can you think of anything else that's just a big blue T?), *Air Raid* was a rumor until 2010: many doubted the game's existence, and didn't even know its real name since the title doesn't appear anywhere on the cart itself.

But in 2010, Tanner Sandlin unearthed a copy of the game in his garage. He put it up for auction and it sold for an incredible $31,600. Since then, more copies have been unearthed, but none have sold for as much as the first one.

RED SEA CROSSING

Year: 1983	Platform: Atari 2600
Rarity: 10/10	Average cost: $13,000

Red Sea Crossing was an obscure game created in 1983 by Steve Stack, made to target Christian households in America. Stack only made a few hundred copies of the game, and they were only distributed via mail order.

There have only been two confirmed copies of the game in circulation. After the first cropped up and sold for $10,400, owners of a curiosities shop in Philadelphia capitalized on the sale by offering their copy up for auction, eventually bringing in a massive $13,877.

SONY

NINTENDO PLAYSTATION

Year: 1992	Platform: N/A
Rarity: 10/10	Average cost: $???

In 1988, Sony made a deal with Nintendo to allow the SNES to use Sony's CD-ROM technology. But the two companies couldn't agree on money issues. This lead to Sony going it alone and establishing the PlayStation brand.

But before they parted, the two companies did come up with a prototype. Apparently 200 were made, each with a SNES cart slot *and* a CD drive installed. It wasn't until 2015 that the consoles were even confirmed to exist. So, now we know that they're real, how much can we expect one to sell for? You'd better start saving up . . .

UNCHARTED 2: FORTUNE HUNTER EDITION

Year: 2009	Platform: PS3
Rarity: 8/10	Average cost: $10,000

This collector's edition was intentionally made to be rare. Sony only ended up producing 200 versions of the edition, and only people that played the demo of *Uncharted 2* during specific weekends in October 2009 were eligible to win a copy.

As collector's editions go, this one is truly something special—the replica dagger in particular is really impressive. As it stands, sealed versions of the game can sell on auction sites for up to $11,000. Open editions tend to go for slightly less, at about $9,000. A real treasure!

ELEMENTAL GEARBOLT ASSASSIN'S CASE

Year: 1998	Platform: PlayStation
Rarity: 10/10	Average cost: $1,500

In 1998 at the Electronic Entertainment Expo in LA, this was given out as a tournament prize. The chest itself is actually more of a briefcase, and it contains a copy of the game, a gold GunCon controller, and a gold PlayStation memory card.

Including employees who were gifted one of these cases, around 40 people managed to score one at the conference. No-one really thought about the game much, until a listing appeared on eBay in 2009, where the game received bids of up to $1,700.

SEGA

SONIC THE HEDGEHOG

Year: 1991	Platform: **Sega Master System**
Rarity: 7/10	Average cost: $500

Here's something interesting about the Sega Master System: the console sold well in Europe, but in Japan and the US, it struggled. In fact, it was Sega's first console flop.

For collectors, that failure was a good thing: it meant very limited amounts of games were produced for the console. One particular game highlights the difference between the European and American success of the console, and that's *Sonic the Hedgehog*: US versions can be worth up to $500, while UK versions of the game (which carry a different barcode) are worth next to nothing.

TETRIS

Year: 1989	Platform: **Sega Genesis**
Rarity: 10/10	Average cost: $10,000

Once upon a time in the eighties, an unlicensed version of *Tetris* on the NES was manufactured and released. It was frowned upon at the time . . . but then Sega came along and developed its own console version to go alongside its System-16 arcade version.

It's unknown how many copies were made before Nintendo shut it down (it had console exclusivity rights at the time), but we know there are at least 10 floating around. The game has been known to sell for up to $16,000 and one even went up with a whopping $1,000,000 price tag!

GENESIS BLOCKBUSTER WORLD VIDEO GAME CHAMPIONSHIPS II

Year: 1995	Platform: **Sega Genesis**
Rarity: 8/10	Average cost: $2,500

Just like Nintendo, Sega also ran its own competitions—the company would tour with special carts and give players that performed particularly well in games like *NBA Jam* and *Judge Dredd* prizes.

This cart is a tough one to track down—estimates suggest there are only two authentic versions of the game out in the wild. It's hard to verify that, because unlike a lot of our other games in this list there are *tons* of reproductions and forgeries of this game on the market.

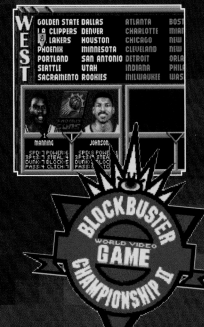

AND THE RAREST OF ALL . . .

BIRTHDAY MANIA

Year:	Platform:
1985	**Atari 2600**
Rarity:	Average cost:
10/10	**$35,000**

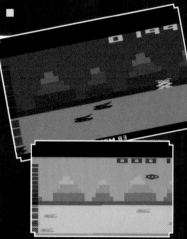

There's only *one* verified copy of this game. It's known to many collectors as the rarest game of all time, thanks to its customizable design. The game itself is pretty simple—players simply pop balloons and blow out candles (a perfect birthday treat).

It's not fully known quite why the game is so rare—we know that not a lot of carts were produced, but it stands to reason that most games got thrown away once people wrote the name of the intended recipient on the box. The only copy out there now has a blank label, and has sold for as much as $35,000.

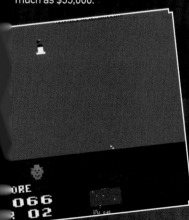

GAMMA ATTACK

Year:	Platform:
1983	**Atari 2600**
Rarity:	Average cost:
10/10	**$???**

We know that a few copies of *Birthday Mania* were produced for the Atari 2600, but it's well documented that only one copy of *Gamma Attack* was ever made. The company that made it—Gammation—has stated this publicly, and the only owner of the game is collector Anthony DeNardo.

DeNardo once listed the game on eBay with a price tag of a whopping $500,000 as a Buy-It-Now, but it didn't sell (hardly surprising!). Being a unique item, though, it could go for anything if DeNardo decides to sell the cart again. You'd better start saving up now, because you never know when it'll go up for sale . . .

THE WORLD'S LARGEST VIDEOGAME COLLECTION

As verified by the *Guinness World Records*, the world's largest video game collection of over 11,000 games was sold on June 16, 2014 for $750,250.

The former owner of the collection—Michael Thomasson—amassed his collection over decades while working in independent gaming stores and running a retail website.

The collection featured over 8,300 complete boxed games, with over 2,600 of them being shrink-wrapped in their original factory packaging. After a heated bidding war, the winner finally took the whole lot for $750,250. That means each game cost an average of $68!

ADVENTURE GAMES

Adventure games might not be the obvious choice when it comes to record-breaking stats. Whether sprawling, single-player experiences, or traditional, point-and-click episodes, adventure games generally don't have you chasing high scores or battling it out for multiplayer supremacy.

Despite this, they can be among the most popular challenges for record-hunters. Those that are massive in scope and offer open-ended ways to play also give inventive gamers the chance to flex their creative muscles; whether that's coming up with ingenious new techniques, exploiting hidden glitches, or mastering heated battles and complex puzzles.

```
          chamber beneath a 3x3 steel grate to th
surface.  A low crawl over cobbles leads inward to the Wes
The grate is open.

You are crawling over cobbles in a low passage.  There is a
dim light at the east end of the passage.
There is a small wicker cage discarded nearby.

> get cage
```

🏆 THE BIGGEST NUMBERS!

A LEGENDARY LEGACY

Though in many ways it's been surpassed by its sequels and legions of imitators, *The Legend of Zelda: Ocarina Of Time* remains the gold standard for adventure games. Its incredible score of **97.54%** on review aggregator GameRankings is still a record for the genre, and places it second on the all-time list.

BUILDING FOR SUCCESS

With dozens of titles released, spanning everything from *Star Wars* to *Harry Potter*, it's no real surprise that Warner Brothers' LEGO games have made well over **$2 billion**. There have been more than **100 million copies sold** so far.

TO (ALMOST) INFINITY AND BEYOND

The universe of *No Man's Sky* is huge, but did you know that the game features an astounding **18.4 quintillion planets**? Even with a supercharged ship visiting one planet every second, it'd still take around **584 million years** to see them all.

IF IT AIN'T BROKEN . . .

When it started life as *Double Fine Adventure* in 2012 with an optimistic goal of **$400,000**, nobody suspected that *Broken Age* would become the largest crowdfunded game to date. **$3.3 million** later, *Broken Age* is Kickstarter's most funded adventure game ever.

BETTER LATE THAN NEVER

Given their size and hefty costs, adventure games often spend years in development. With *The Last Guardian*, director Fumito Ueda and Team Ico took things to the extreme. It took almost **11 years to complete**, longer than any other adventure game, and completely missing the entire PS3 generation.

EXPLORING THE LIMITS

The Witness is a tough game to master and its ultimate test can frustrate even expert players. *The Challenge* is a series of the game's trademark maze puzzles set against a tight time limit. The catch? They're randomly generated, so there's no way to fully prepare for what you are about to face. That didn't stop speedrunner RbdJellyfish though, who managed to face down *The Challenge* in a world-record time of 1m 43s. Yikes!

HUNGRY LIKE THE WOLF

C lover Studio's brilliant action-adventure game **Okami** is an all-time favorite, and has been a staple of the speedrunning scene for years. This is thanks, in part, to its gorgeous art style and distinctive Celestial Brush gameplay, but also because there is a wealth of shortcuts for record-breakers to exploit.

The most competitive *Okami* record is its New Game+ speedrun; a title that's changed hands many times. To put together the ideal run, players need to master the Karmic Transformer glitch, which lets Amaterasu jump infinitely—as long as you can nail the timing down to the frame. Speedrunner lEternalDarkness has managed this. Through overcoming invisible walls and skipping entire levels, his time of **1h 22m 39s** has become the one to beat.

+10.0
+4.0
+13.0
+6.5
+8.9
-2.2
+3.1

-0.

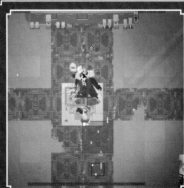

RUSHING THE RUSH

I t's easy to focus just on how it looks, but there's way more to **Hyper Light Drifter** than its pretty pixel-art. Fast-paced action, satisfying combat, and a mysterious world are some of the things that make this indie action-adventure a gem, but its challenging bosses are also a real highlight. Boasting devastating attacks that require dexterity to avoid, downing them is no mean feat.

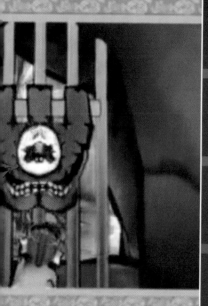

IT'S DANGEROUS TO GO ALONE . . .

Part of the appeal of the original *The Legend of Zelda* on the NES was its sense of mystery, as you were dropped in the middle of Hyrule with no directions, no items, and no advice besides the words of an old man telling you: "It's dangerous to go alone!" Reading this phrase would prompt Link to pick up his sword—his first line of defense against a world teeming with monsters—but in the search for record-breaking glory, some hardy gamers have chosen to ignore even this most basic weapon.

Making it all the way to the end of the game without picking up *any* items (besides bombs) is what we call an "extreme" run of *The Legend of Zelda*. Only a few experts have achieved this amazing feat in good time. The current record of **1h 25m 24s** was set by speedrunner LackAttack24 in 2015.

The Legend of Zelda Extreme%		15/107	
	+/-	Time	vs. gold
Exit 2	-17.1	3:14	-17.6
Bow	-30.7	5:40	-19
1st Board	-63.6	7:47	-10.8
Wand	-3.66	13:32	-6 a
3rd Board	-1.24	17:56	-11.8
4th Board	+58.2	22:27	-27 9
2nd Board		24:46	-1.40
5th Board		31:46	
7th Board		42:59	
Reach "Gannon"		1:30:19	
		23:51.53	
	3:52.46		1:24.43
	3:06.17		
Possible Time Save			12.88
Sum of Best Segments			1:21:32
Comparing Against			Personal Best
Total Playtime			1d 6:19:25

Fortunately, developer Heart Machine included a Boss Rush mode, and mastering the complexities of the game's powerful enemies has proven a popular challenge. You need to run this gauntlet in a matter of minutes if you want to make it anywhere near the top of the leaderboard. The record belongs to streamer Auriorious, whose time of **3m 11s 23ms** looks pretty tough to beat!

Console-exclusive Skylanders grow the number of characters even more!

SOME MAJOR FIGURES

Though it's not a player-set landmark, Activision has made sure that *Skylanders* is the franchise to beat when it comes to toys-to-life records. It makes sense, as the series was the first to really popularize the genre, but that doesn't make the volume of Skylanders available any less impressive.

From the release of *Spyro's Adventure* in 2011 through to 2016's *Imaginators*, a staggering **258 main Skylanders figures** have been released. And that's without even counting the hundreds of special items, vehicles, and variants! So, while you're unlikely to run out of new LEGO *Dimensions* characters, and Nintendo won't be slowing down its amiibo releases any time soon, both have a long way to go if they want to match *Skylanders* for sheer choice and variety.

BREATHTAKING ZELDA RECORDS!

Not only is *The Legend of Zelda: Breath of the Wild* one of the greatest adventure games ever made, it's also a goldmine for record-hunters. Since the game's release, dozens of records have been set and smashed as players continue to discover new ways to shave off crucial seconds from their times. New record categories keep springing up too, so there are always fresh and interesting challenges to try. With a flexible main quest, hundreds of collectibles, and plenty of skillful tricks and techniques to master, gamers will be making and breaking records for years to come.

ANY % COMPLETION
Time: 39m 57s

The rules are simple: get to the castle and defeat **Calamity Ganon** as quickly as possible. Ikkitrix's time comes down to a mastery of the Whistle Sprinting and Shield Jumping techniques, though they had help from an amiibo-spawned horse on the way.

ALL DUNGEONS COMPLETION
Time: 2h 09m 46s

Most take dozens of hours to beat the main quests. To do it in just over two is outrageous! Speedrunner atz managed it, thanks to ingenious use of the Stasis rune—using crates, boulders, and logs to send Link flying across the map.

Every second counts when chasing records—there's barely even time to fight!

MASTER SWORD REAL TIME ATTACK
Time: 2h 13m 06s

What makes Cookiepocolypse's race to get the Master Sword so impressive? It's not just a case of getting to the right location. The speedrunner had to complete a lengthy list of tasks first, fitting all of these into a run of just over two hours.

LINK BY NUMBERS

125
DIFFERENT WEAPONS
that Link can wield, from brittle Boko Bats to the legendary Master Sword.

33
SHIELDS
available in the game, to be swiped from enemies or even found in hidden treasure chests.

900
KOROK SEEDS
to find in the vast expanse of Hyrule; the biggest *Zelda* side quest ever!

75
PIECES OF UNIQUE ARMOR
to collect, including exclusive sets that are unlocked using special amiibo.

1,385,000
COPIES OF BREATH OF THE WILD
sold across both Switch and Wii U in the first month in the US alone, making it the fastest-selling *Zelda* ever.

120
SHRINES TO COMPLETE
along with the five main dungeons—more than any other *Zelda* game.

97
BREATH OF THE WILD'S METASCORE
which is the highest of any Wii U or Switch game and good for 12th on the all-time list.

61
SQUARE KILOMETERS
is the (rough) size of *Breath of the Wild's* map, dwarfing all previous *Zelda* games and even bettering *Horizon*!

8 TOP TIPS

HOW TO BREAK RECORDS

Napstablook	−1.8 1:49
Toriel	4:55
enter snowdin	8:52
papyrus	12:07
enter nice cream man room	14:36

2:38.97

2:38.97

49.47

PB: 3:04.50	
Best: 3:04.50	
Previous Segment	−1.8
Possible Time Save	0.00
Best Possible Time	14:28
Sum of Best Segments	14:28
Total Playtime	1:38:51

1 PICK YOUR GAME

General skills such as menu speed, item usage, and general coordination will help in some adventure games. But, if you want to set records then you need to focus in on a specific game. Choose one game and stick at it.

3 KNOW YOUR GLITCHES

In speedrunning, glitches are your friends—essential tools that can help shave off crucial seconds or even create entirely new routes through games. If you really want to master your game of choice, do your research, and start taking shortcuts.

JustinDM

Metroid Prime Any%

Space Jump	5:45
Zoid Start	10:00
Zoid End	11:15
Varia	15:48
Wild	17:48
Boost	21:16
Wave + Sun	24:24
HOOoOOOoOOOOoOO...	31:36
X-Ray	-
Plasma	40:11
Spirit	42:02
Thermal	46:09
Main PBs	50:24
Suit	-
Warrior	59:03
World	1:02:31
Ridley	1:06:30
Exo	1:12:42
Essence	1:14:19
Previous Segment	
Possible Time Save	17
Sum of Best	1:10:44

05:59:88

2 STUDY THE PROS

You can watch thousands of record-breaking videos by the world's best players online and many of them are happy to share their secrets, too. Take the time to seek out breakdowns and tutorials from your favorite streamers—then make sure you use those skills to break your own records!

4 OUTSIDE THE BOX

Most records are broken by refining tried and tested methods. If you really want to make a name for yourself though, try coming up with exciting new approaches—like one of the various sequence breaks made famous by *Metroid* speedrunners. Just because nobody's tried it before, doesn't mean it won't work!

5 BREAKING GROUND

A good place to start is where there are no rivals to overhaul. Invent new categories for popular games, or be the first to lay down the gauntlet on an underrepresented adventure title. A record's a record, after all.

6 DIVIDE & CONQUER

Even rapid speedruns on some of the lengthiest adventure games can take many hours to complete. To make the most of your time, it's a good idea to split the game into chunks, and then focus on the most challenging sections to hone your skills.

7 PLAY TO YOUR STRENGTHS

Adventure games will test your combat, platforming, piloting, and puzzle-solving skills to the limit, but there's nothing that says you need to master them all. If you're struggling with a game, just play to your strengths and specialize in one skill.

8 NEW HORIZONS

While it's fun to replay classics, there are amazing new adventure games being released all the time. Go for records on new releases for a fresh challenge—and for a chance to propel yourself to the top of the leaderboards.

TRAINING GAMES

THE LEGEND OF ZELDA: BREATH OF THE WILD

Ideal for massive adventures and short runs alike.

HORIZON: ZERO DAWN

The perfect adventure game in which to hone your bow, trap, and melee combat skills.

THE WITNESS

Perfect for testing out your spatial reasoning and lateral thinking skills, it is packed with head-scratchers to mull over.

LEGO DIMENSIONS

Levels filled with collectibles, characters with different playstyles, and races in vehicles across land, sea, and air.

STREET IGHTER II

The most influential fighting game of all time, and still great fun to play today! This one-on-one game is regarded as one of the true industry greats, and the original SNES release remains Capcom's third most successful title ever, even 25 years later! With a varied cast of characters (which has grown massively over the years through numerous sequels) and cool special moves, *Street Fighter II* set the standard for every fighter that has come along since.

The original game launched with **just 8** playable characters. Fast-forward to *Ultra Street Fighter IV* and that roster has grown to a whopping **44**.

Across hundreds of sequels, spin-offs, and cameos, *Street Fighter* hero Ryu has gone toe-to-toe with almost **700** different characters!

INSERT COIN

BLANKA

By 1995, Street Fighter II arcade machines had taken **$2.3 billion**. That works out at over 9 billion quarters pumped into cabinets by eager players!

The 1992 SNES release is the best-selling game in the series, with over **6.3 million** copies sold.

In the last year alone, pro Street Fighter tournaments handed out over **$1 million** in prize money.

HARDWARE HEAVEN

DEVICES THAT PUSHED THE LIMITS

The world of video game development is an ever-changing and fast-evolving one. That's part of what makes it so exciting, and in this section we are going take a look at the pieces of gaming hardware that broke the mold and established their own mind-blowing records.

We've delved deep into video game history to find some of the coolest, most interesting, successful, and just plain weird pieces of hardware ever produced. From the first home console ever made, to the best-selling gaming system ever; from the smallest handheld, to the most complicated controller your eyes will ever gaze upon; from a Game Boy that can survive an actual *warzone*, to the founding father of video games; come pay homage to these feats and take a trip into the Hardware Hall of Fame.

Did You Know?

The world's largest arcade machine stands 14.5 feet (4.4m) tall. Built by gaming enthusiast Jason Camberis, the gigantic machine plays over 250 classic games!

THE KING OF CONSOLES

Many have tried to take its crown, but the PS2 is still the king of console sales. The stylish black box sold more than **154 million units** worldwide—that's more than enough to give three to every single person in California right now. And you'd still have a cool 30 million consoles spare!

WHERE IT ALL BEGAN

Video games have been around since the 1950s, though back then they were more like mini experiments built by scientists than games that you'd play at home with your friends. But, in 1972, the Magnavox Odyssey arrived into homes as the **first "modern" games console** with swappable games. The Odyssey changed everything, and it kickstarted a phenomenon that continues to this day, 45 years later.

The Virtual Boy will go down in history as an interesting-looking migraine machine!

GREAT THINGS IN SMALL PACKAGES

The 2000s were a time when devices were just getting smaller and smaller. There were phones the size of belt buckles and teeny handheld consoles, like the **Pokémon Mini**. The teeny cuboid is a mere 2.9 x 2.3 x 0.9 inches (74 x 58 x 23 mm), the **smallest handheld gaming machine ever made**.

THE BIGGEST BANK-BREAKER

You might not have heard of the 3DO, and there's a good reason for that: the console came out in 1993 and was a spectacular failure. In three years it barely racked up two million sales. Not only was it awful, it cost an astronomical price—**$699 ($1,165 in today's money)**—and it wasn't even very good!

HEAVY HITTER

On its debut, the PS3 was a powerhouse, and it looked the part. The system was big and imposing, and it spewed out heat from its fan like a dragon. What definitely caught people off guard, however, was how heavy the thing was. Weighing in at 5KG, the original **PS3 is the heaviest gaming console released**. Luckily, Sony put later versions of the console on a diet.

THE MOST COMPLICATED CONTROLLER EVER

Back in the 8-bit computer days, most joysticks only had a single button!

Though today's controllers have come a long way from the simple two-button pads used by early consoles, they're still pretty easy to work out. Playing a game should be easier than piloting a plane, right? Well, Capcom didn't think so when it made its hulking mech action game *Steel Battalion*, and it made an *extraordinary* controller to go with the game's release. Just look at that thing: two joysticks, throttle, a sea of buttons and . . . pedals!? By far the most complicated controller you will ever see. Now, who can find the "start" button?

MOST POWERFUL HANDHELD

Some people argue that the Nintendo Switch is a home console and it doesn't deserve the title of "Most Powerful Handheld," but those people are wrong. Can you take it out with you? Can you play it on a bus? Can you *hold and play it in your five-fingered hands*? Yes, you can. And that makes the Switch the most powerful portable gaming console.

> **Can you play it on a bus? Can you hold and play it in your five-fingered hands? Yes, you can.**

GAMING'S FIRST VR SYSTEM . . . SORT OF

Virtual Reality is seen as the future of gaming, but this current wave of VR headsets wasn't strictly the first. "VR" actually hit homes in 1994 with the Virtual Boy, a "portable" console from Nintendo. The world wasn't ready for the Virtual Boy though, and so as well as being the first "VR" home console, it holds a joint record for being Nintendo's biggest flop. It only displayed two colors (red and black), no game developer wanted to make games for it, and it gave people headaches. Take it from us, this is one instance where VR was definitely *not* the future of gaming.

The Virtual Boy was Nintendo's least successful hardware release ever!

Neo-Geo games are some of the most expensive in the world!

THE BIGGEST GAMES

There's nothing like sliding a new disk into your PS4 or Xbox One and watching it be slowly devoured by the console, or neatly tucking a game card into your switch and hearing that satisfying "click". Another feeling that never, ever, gets old is whacking a Neo-Geo cartridge into its holster. Why? Well, because the actual games themselves were so massive. At 7.5 x 5.4 inches (190 x 136 mm) they will probably forever stand as (literally) the biggest games ever made.

THE GRANDFATHER OF VIDEO GAMES

We wouldn't be even talking about modern video games if it weren't for their founding father, Ralph Baer. He's famous for designing the Magnavox Odyssey, the very first home console. Without Baer's invention, gaming could've been very different. Ralph passed away in 2014; however, he has left a legacy that has endured for 45 years.

BULLETPROOF

Some objects just refuse to break: cast iron pans, memory sticks, and, of course: the original Game Boy. Nintendo's portable was as thick as a brick, so it felt pretty hardy in your hand, and it could survive a good fall . . . but that's only the beginning. During the Gulf War in 1991, an American GI took his Game Boy on deployment. Unfortunately, he was attacked. He made it through, but his handheld had taken some significant damage and looked melted. But, after some tinkering and a set of new batteries, it sprung to life. Don't try anything like *that* at home though.

MULTIPLAYER

It's fun to go after records on your own and get all the glory, but sometimes it's even better to share the triumph with some friends. Working together to bring down that next big boss, or using each other's special skills to smash through a level in record time feels awesome.

From highly organized raid teams in games like *Destiny* to lone wolves speeding along the tracks of *Mario Kart*, multiplayer games come in many different shapes and sizes, so knowing the best way to tackle each title is a must. And, we've got the perfect introduction to all that right here.

LEAGUE OF LEGENDS
This MOBA is the biggest free-to-play game on PC, with over **65 million** players a month and over **25 million** of those playing daily!

Did You Know?

Over 8,962,000 players have created their own Guardians in *Destiny* since it launched in 2014.

🏆 THE BIGGEST NUMBERS!

THE HIGHEST SCORE

Rocket League has made **$110 million** but cost just $2 million to make. The game has awarded **$530,962** in prize money over **129 tournaments**, too—not bad considering it was originally offered for free!

DAWN OF THE AWESOME!

Dota 2 is a popular MOBA that attracts millions of players who compete in massive tournaments. The most recent prize pool was a massive **$20,770,640** and the winning team took home **$9,139,002**!

A GROWING CROWD

eSports audiences are estimated to be over **238,100,000 million** as of the end of 2016. That means that eSports are worth a staggering **$1,130,000,000** across all games and tournaments!

WHAT A WEEK

The hugely popular *Overwatch* managed to get **over one million people** playing the game in the week it launched. That meant people spent more than **119 million hours** on the game that week!

A WHOLE DECADE!

Destiny—a multiplayer game about defeating aliens and taking their precious loot—was released in 2014, and publisher Activision has dedicated **$500 million** to the project, which will span new games and stories for an **unprecedented 10 years!**

NEW KID ON THE BLOCK

Overwatch launched in 2016 to critical acclaim and shook up the whole multiplayer community. In no time at all it became the go-to game for competitive play, instantly challenging long-established multiplayer classics like *League Of Legends*, *Destiny*, and many more. Here are the most impressive stats from *Overwatch's* first year on the scene . . .

9.7 MILLION
players took part in the game's beta

EARNED
$1,000,000,000
in less than a year

Attracted more than
30,000,000
players across all platforms

119,000,000
hours clocked up in the game's first week

MORE THAN
100
Game of the Year awards received

COMPETITION: DESTROYED!

MOST PLAYERS ONLINE IN A SINGLE FPS

In January 2015, Sony Online Entertainment teamed up with a community of *PlanetSide 2* players to organize one of the biggest social gaming events ever. After lots of planning, Sony and the community managed to attract a massive **1,158 players** into the same match at the same time.

LONGEST MARATHON HALO RUN

Back in October 2015, to celebrate the launch of *Halo 5*, Paavo 'Paavi' Niskala managed to clock an impressive **50 hours, 4 minutes, and 17 seconds** playing through the *Halo* series. That's over two days straight of nothing but *Halo*!

Halo is one of the most successful multiplayer games ever, helping to shape how the FPS genre works as an eSport.

GAMING'S LARGEST SPACE BATTLE

Sci-fi MMO *EVE Online* has a habit of breaking records, and it currently has **60,000 players** constantly battling it out for space supremacy. Two in-game sectors—the CFC and the Imperium—are attracting players who are always competing for control of in-game trading routes, planets, and more.

SMASHING THE COMPETITION!

Gonzalo "ZeRo" Barrios currently holds the record for winning the most *Super Smash Bros.* tournaments in a row. Barrios won **53 Super Smash Bros. tournaments** without being dethroned between November 2014 and October 2015, before his streak finally came to an end in the Smash World Finals of 2015.

MOST PLAYERS IN A MULTIPLAYER TOURNAMENT

EA's *FIFA* Interactive World Cup attracted more players than ever before in 2013: **2,500,000 players signed up** to the competition, and over a grueling few weeks they were whittled down to just the 21 best players, who all got to play the Finals live in Madrid.

HISTORY OF THE WORLD (OF WARCRAFT)

The total time the 100 million lifetime players of *World of Warcraft* have spent in the game is longer than the existence of the human race! If the total times are added together, it comes to more than 50,000,000,000 hours—roughly **5.9 million years**. The game has also made over $10 billion from its player base.

FIRST EVER MULTIPLAYER GAME

The first ever multiplayer game wasn't online; it wasn't played by two players with separate controllers or anything like that. No, it was made **way back in 1952** by Alexander S. Douglas, and was called *OXO*. It was an electronic version of tic-tac-toe, and built on a calculator that you could pass between your friends. This was the start of video games as we know them.

THE BIGGEST GAMING EVENTS

FANS COME TOGETHER IN RECORD NUMBERS!

MINECON

The largest convention based around a single game, Minecon (yes, you guessed it, it's all about *Minecraft*) attracts fans from around the world. It's held in a different place every year, and it has already visited Las Vegas, Paris, and London. Getting tickets is nearly impossible. In 2013, the first wave sold out in three seconds!

Did You Know?

ComicCons like Penny Arcade Expo (US) and MCM (UK) aren't just for comics and movies—there's always plenty of gaming stuff to see and do at these events, too!

WINGS GAMING
TI6 Champions

THE INTERNATIONAL

This is the final event of the *Dota 2* competitive calendar each year and the best place to see the highest level of play. Prize pools have been getting increasingly crazy—2017's event gave away almost $25 million in prize money, way up from the first event's $2 million. Tens of millions watch the tournament live online.

E3

This is more of an industry convention than a fan one. Still, in recent years, E3 has opened its doors to members of the public, giving lucky visitors the chance to play the best upcoming games. Nearly 70,000 people attended the Los Angeles convention in 2016, with 15,000 of those being members of the public.

GAMESCOM

Held every summer in Cologne, Germany, Gamescom is sort of the European version of E3. Despite E3 being the main event on the gaming calendar, Gamescom is actually bigger. Attendance figures in recent years have been just shy of 350,000 per year, and lines to play the hottest new games can be hours long!

LEAGUE OF LEGENDS WORLD CHAMPIONSHIP

League's equivalent of The International might not have the ludicrous prize pools of Valve's competition, but it smashes it in terms of viewership! Prize pools are still in the millions but the World Championship is an eSports event that has been known to attract more viewers than even some real-life sporting events.

GAMES DONE QUICK

A week-long charity speedrun marathon that happens twice a year, with Awesome Games Done Quick in January and Summer Games Done Quick anywhere between May and August. For seven grueling days, hundreds of players smash through games in record time, playing 24 hours a day in front of packed halls and for hundreds of thousands of viewers online.

SIGMA
18:32

ORI AND THE BLIND FOREST

tiny
build

BANDAI
NAMCO
Entertainment

PRIZES
VALLU
1:05:18

SUPER MARIO GALAXY 2
Wii 2010
$972,680

Provided by Christopher Delamente
Super Mario Grey Goomba Dot Art

THE EXPERT SAYS . . .

VULAJIN, GAMES DONE QUICK STAFF

For a GDQ, the process of picking games is complex. Our overall goals are to produce a schedule that will raise money for our charity partner; that will entertain viewers; and that will represent a cross-section of what the community has to offer. A lot of factors go into this process beyond "does this runner/game have name recognition?" We try to pick a wide array of games to attract a diverse audience. We also try to showcase games that people might not realize make for fun watches. Speedrunners of popular series like *Mario*, *Mega Man*, and *Zelda* will always be represented.

GAMES
INDIE

In a world of big names and endless sequels and spin-offs, it's indie games that are arguably pushing the world of gaming to new heights. From painting the world around you in *The Unfinished Swan* to exploring the biggest game universe (literally) in *No Man's Sky*, the indiesphere is where the most interesting and unusual gaming experiences are.

Of course, that means there is a near-endless list of gaming records in the realm of indie games. Sublime speedruns, insanely-difficult bosses, pixel-perfect leaps . . . you name it, they have it. Indie games are rich pickings for gaming record-hunters.

Rocket League is constantly updated with extra stuff, including new modes and arenas.

Did You Know?

The term "indie game" has been around since gaming began, with many legendary game-makers starting off coding from their bedrooms.

🏆 THE BIGGEST NUMBERS!

MOST SEQUELS

Indie developers tend to move onto something new once they've made a game. Sequels aren't really a big thing in the indie game community . . . with one main exception. Scott Cawthon's *Five Nights at Freddy's* series has a **stream of sequels**—four in fact, developed in only two years.

MIGHTY MINECRAFT

You've heard of *Minecraft*, right? Of course you have; you'd have to have lived in a cave for the last ten years to not have heard of **Mojang's massive monolith**. It's by far the most successful indie game ever, selling over a mind-blowing **120 million** copies.

MOST DESIRABLE INDIE STUDIO

It comes as no surprise that the most desirable maker of indie games is the maker of the most popular indie game ever made, *Minecraft*. **Mojang** was bought by Microsoft for **$2.5 billion**, making it the most expensive acquisition of any indie game studio ever.

A UNIVERSE OF POSSIBILITIES

There aren't many games that can boast that they have **18 quintillion planets** (that's 18,446,744,073,709,551,616 planets, to be exact) to explore. In fact, there's only one: *No Man's Sky*. Crazier still, this gigantic game was built by a small development team of only about 16 people!

KICKSTARTER KILLER

The likes of *Yooka-Laylee* and *Mighty No. 9* were made possible thanks to successful Kickstarter crowdfunding campaigns, but they pale in comparison to the runaway champion that is *Shenmue III*. **$6.3 million** was pledged by fans on its Kickstarter campaign alone!

ndie games have seen
a fair amount of support
from the big-hitters.
Recently, both Sony and
Microsoft have taken a
number of fledgling
studios under their wing
and helped to launch their
games into your home—
No Man's Sky and
Cuphead are both
examples of this.
However, no studio has
supported indie games
more than Devolver
Digital, which has made
a name for itself by
publishing a ton of indie
classics, such as *Enter
the Gungeon*, *OlliOlli*,
Luftrausers, and *Titan
Souls*. Thank you!

⚡ INCREDIBLE FEATS!

BIGGEST ISN'T ALWAYS BEST

BORE OFF BLOODSHED

Indie gaming is where some of the most creative stuff happens. In most RPGs (think *Final Fantasy* or *Dragon Quest*), a battle is inevitable: at some point, you're going to have to defeat a foe. That's not the case with **Undertale**, though.

This is the only RPG where you can play through the entire game **without killing anything**—not even raising your hand against your enemy. That's pretty impressive, and the game doesn't get boring if you do choose to go down the path of the pacifist. You even get the game's best ending for being such a good person.

Unique combat options such as "Talk" and "Mercy" really make *Undertale* special.

* Froggit and

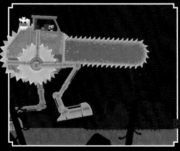

MOST SPEEDRUNNERS

What's the most hotly-contested indie game for speedrunning? *Super Meat Boy*? *Braid*? *Fez*? Try again . . . it's actually the pacifism-loving, off-kilter RPG **Undertale** that's the most popular indie game battleground for speedrunners. With **444 players** actively climbing over one another in order to be the fastest across a bunch of categories, it only *just* beats *Super Meat Boy*'s 436. It also wins in terms of number of actual speedruns—2,360 attempts, once again just beating out *Super Meat Boy*'s 2,005.

ALL TIME

Many indie games get a lot of love on release, but what is the highest rated indie game of recent years? You can stop naming games now—you're probably not going to guess it. In the face of stiff competition, it's the Wii version of **World of Goo** that comes out on top. With a **Metascore of 94**, it is the highest-rated indie game, beating the likes of other indie darlings such as classics like *Braid* (93) and *Fez* (91), as well as modern classics, including *Overwatch* (91) and *Batman: Arkham City* (also at 91).

RUNAWAY SUCCESS

It's unsurprising that a game so straightforward would appeal to a lot of gamers. Still, **Rocket League** surpassed its developer's expectations, becoming an overnight success thanks in part to it being given away for free on Sony's Playstation Plus service. Once word spread about *Rocket League*, everyone wanted a piece of the action. Today, the game has **30 million registered players**, its own eSports league, and a host of DLC packages—both free and paid. Back of the net, Psyonix!

drew near!

Being a game about sweeping, you'd think that *Dustforce* would be boring. Trust us, it's not!

BIGGEST BRAIN-BENDER

Jonathan Blow. That's the name you're going to keep muttering to yourself whenever you get stuck on **The Witness**'s mind-bending puzzles. It requires you to think differently to how you would in real life. Blow, the architect of the game, is like a supervillain of gaming. His power? An unmatched intellect, and the ability to make anyone clutch their head in anguish when stumped by a difficult puzzle.

THE HOTTEST INDIE GAMES TO FINISH FAST

MINECRAFT

CHALLENGES
- Navigating menus
- Learning the world seed
- Accounting for randomness

TOP 3 RUNNERS
- xTheeSizzler (7m 17s)
- illumina1337 (7m 57s)
- Funderful1000 (8m 20s)

We're taking a look at seeded *Minecraft* here, so you know what you're getting into before you start. That said, you still have to contend with not knowing where an enemy may be lurking before you drop down into a mine. This run is a tough one to run, but rewarding once you get it down.

UNDERTALE

CHALLENGES
- Dodging attacks
- Random encounters
- A lot of RNG

TOP 3 RUNNERS
- TGH (56m 32s)
- Xandertje10 (56m 32s)
- Magolor9000 (57m 08s)

This being a standard (well, sort of) RPG, it has random encounters which can really mess up your run if the RNG gods are not on your side. It's also quicker to run away from battles, which is also down to RNG. Basically, you have to cross your fingers and hope you get lucky if you're thinking about running this game.

ANTICHAMBER

CHALLENGES
- Learning the game world
- Perfect positioning
- Need good aim

TOP 3 RUNNERS
- xHF01x (44s 920ms)
- CAKEbuilder (45s 580ms)
- gizmovor (47s 050ms)

Speedrunning *Antichamber* kind of changes the genre of the entire game from a mind-bending puzzler to a twitch platformer. To finish this at a perfect time, you need to perfectly learn the game in order to be at the exact right place at precisely the right time. Get that down and you can finish the game in under a minute!

Antichamber is usually hard, but the speedrun route skips pretty much the entire game!

SUPER MEAT BOY

CHALLENGES
- Pixel-perfect jumping
- Learning the levels
- Hotly contested leaderboards

TOP 3 RUNNERS
- Hamb (17m 41s)
- Vorpal (17m 43s)
- Zaxt (17m 55s)

Super Meat Boy is perfect for speedrunning, and its quick respawn time when you die means that you can afford the occasional death or two. That said, the game's been around for a while, so quite a lot of runners have gotten playing the game down to a fine art, making it hard to beat out the competition.

SHOVEL KNIGHT

CHALLENGES
- ★ Bouncing on enemies perfectly
- ★ Not wasting time doubling back on yourself
- ★ Steep difficulty curve

TOP 3 RUNNERS
- ★ Smaugy (42m 54s)
- ★ MooMooAkai (43m 42s)
- ★ MunchaKoopas (43m 49s)

This game has been designed to be like an old-school 8-bit platformer, and if you've happened to play the original *Super Mario Bros.*, you'll know that those games were *hard*. *Shovel Knight* plays homage to that difficulty, and the game is hard enough before you even factor in playing it perfectly and quickly.

SUPERHOT

CHALLENGES
- ★ Learning enemy movement
- ★ Making every step count
- ★ Perfect aim

TOP 3 RUNNERS
- ★ Bulletts (18m 18s)
- ★ Lt_Disco (19m 31s)
- ★ Ellieceraptor (19m 47s)

As the world only moves when you move, you can plan the optimal path for *Superhot* ahead of time. You can do all the planning in the world, but it'll mean nothing if you don't have the skill to back it up, so you still need to practice like crazy to even think about getting this run done quick.

ORI AND THE BLIND FOREST

CHALLENGES
- ★ Obtaining power-ups quickly
- ★ Avoiding enemies
- ★ Navigating menus

TOP 3 RUNNERS
- ★ Ikewolf (22m 34s)
- ★ a515505156 (23m 27s)
- ★ ssjhenrik (23m 56s)

It's something you don't think about until you start considering speedrunning a game, but navigating a game's menus can eat up a lot of your time. In *Ori and the Blind Forest*, you have a skill tree and you need to know the correct inputs perfectly in order to minimize your times—much like a cheat code, actually.

DUSTFORCE DX

CHALLENGES
- ★ Pixel-perfect jumping
- ★ Need to mop up all dust on each level
- ★ Building up special move

TOP 3 RUNNERS
- ★ Sivade (56m 11s)
- ★ Dice (57m 00s)
- ★ ciwb (57m 08s)

Dustforce demands a high level of skill to play properly from the get-go, so running through all the levels at the fastest speed possible is a *big* ask. That said, it is actually a pretty relaxing and satisfying game once you get your tactics down, and it's a pretty rewarding game to speedrun as well.

Super Metroid has been run at every Games Done Quick event since it began in 2010—that's **18 charity runs** in just seven years.

SUPER METROID

Nintendo's superb 16-bit adventure game laid out the template for what is now known as "Metroidvania," games centered around exploring huge maps and using the power-ups earned to reach new locations. It's one of the biggest games on the speedrunning scene, as well as being held up as an example of one of the very best games of its era. It's playable today on both the SNES Mini and Virtual Console.

There are a total of **100** power-up items to be found, ranging from new weapons and abilities to ammo and health upgrades.

The epic adventure was developed by a small team of just **15** talented people.

28m
Fastest in-game completion time with no major glitches, tied by Oatsngoats and zoast.

Super Metroid is one of the highest-rated games on aggregation site gamerankings.com, with an average review score of **95.5%**.

THE CRAZIEST RECORDS OF ALL TIME

CASTLEVANIA
SYMPHONY OF THE NIGHT BLINDFOLDED

Castlevania: Symphony Of The Night is a challenging game, thanks largely to its confusing level design and army of difficult bosses. So when famed speedrunner Romscout set out to beat the game blindfolded, nobody actually expected that he'd be able to do it—it should be an impossible task. But then again, there aren't many players out there with muscle memory like Romscout. It took just 54 minutes for him to defeat Dracula and win a place in the record books.

SUPER MARIO 64
1.2 STARS PER MINUTE!?

The popularity of perfect platformer *Super Mario 64* has led many fans to invest themselves in learning all its secrets and shortcuts. One of our favorite records is the 120-star challenge, a 100% completion run that grabs every Power Star in the game. Competitive runners cheese05 and Puncayshun are two of the finest SM64 players in the world, with cheese05 running this landmark release in just 1 hour, 39 minutes, and 28 seconds.

VARIOUS GAMES
CONTROLLER INSANITY

Some games are known for being super difficult, but that has pushed some players to beat them in unusual ways. The record for the craziest has to go to Benjamin "Bearzly" Gwin. The Canadian gamer has completed some of the world's hardest games repeatedly, using some bizarre controllers. That includes the *Rock Band* guitar, the *Donkey Konga* bongo set, a dance mat, and even a microphone (using his voice to control every action).

WORLD OF WARCRAFT
TRUE NEUTRAL

If you want to have a chance of survival in Azeroth, you need to pick a side. Or so we thought. Starting as a Pandaren in *World of Warcraft*, you begin the game as a neutral player, choosing between Alliance or Horde when you leave the starting area. But Doubleagent never left the starting area, deciding to stick to the Wandering Isles as a neutral player instead. It took 4,152 hours to grind through to the former level cap of 90. Now *that's* dedication to setting a world record . . .

SUPER MARIO GALAXY 2
FREEFALL GAMING

When Jesse Moerkerk climbed into an indoor skydiving tunnel, he set out to earn his place in gaming history: the longest gaming session in freefall. For 18 minutes and 52 seconds, Moerkerk could be found suspended in a vertical tunnel, with the wind in his hair and a Wiimote in hand. Not only did he manage to play *Super Mario Galaxy 2* in these conditions without throwing up, he also managed to complete the first boss level. It's a feat that is unlikely to ever be beaten because it's completely crazy!

EVE ONLINE

THE BATTLE OF B-R5RB

Back in 2014, the largest ever player versus player battle in the history of gaming took place, and it was all because one player forgot to pay a routine space station maintenance bill. 2,670 players—more than 7,548 characters—flooded into the B-R5RB system to vie for control of the station. The ensuing battle lasted for over 21 consecutive hours, racking up losses in-game of over 11 trillion ISK—that's a theoretical real world value of around $300,000.

ENERGY 99

MINECRAFT

GET CONNECTED WITH STEVE

Players have done some impressive things in *Minecraft* over the years, but perhaps the finest comes from Jordan "CaptainSparklez" Maron. Teaming up with Verizon, Maron was able to build a working telephone within *Minecraft*, capable of browsing the web and making actual video calls—with the caller's face rendered in blocks. It's actually pretty incredible—you can even take selfies of your avatar with the in-game device and send them out into the world. It's a truly amazing thing to see!

Sunny OK   Happy GOOD   Funky OK   Crazy PERFECT   Baby GOOD

JUST DANCE

MONSTER DANCE SESSION

Dancing games are great fun when you want to just have fun with friends. But they can also be used to test your endurance, mental strength, and capacity to groove to catchy pop music. Carrie Swidecki set an impressive marathon record when she danced for 138 hours and 34 seconds on *Just Dance 2015*. Millions were watching on Twitch, and she raised $7,305 for charity—sore legs were a small price to pay for such a victory.

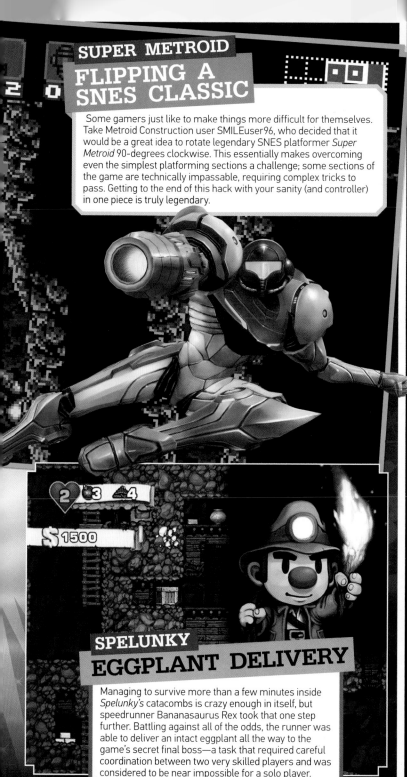

SUPER METROID
FLIPPING A SNES CLASSIC

Some gamers just like to make things more difficult for themselves. Take Metroid Construction user SMILEuser96, who decided that it would be a great idea to rotate legendary SNES platformer *Super Metroid* 90-degrees clockwise. This essentially makes overcoming even the simplest platforming sections a challenge; some sections of the game are technically impassable, requiring complex tricks to pass. Getting to the end of this hack with your sanity (and controller) in one piece is truly legendary.

SPELUNKY
EGGPLANT DELIVERY

Managing to survive more than a few minutes inside *Spelunky's* catacombs is crazy enough in itself, but speedrunner Bananasaurus Rex took that one step further. Battling against all of the odds, the runner was able to deliver an intact eggplant all the way to the game's secret final boss—a task that required careful coordination between two very skilled players and was considered to be near impossible for a solo player.

GET CRAZY!

5 WAYS TO AMP UP YOUR RECORDS

One-handed
Want to set your own records? Try playing the most difficult game in your library with just one hand. Better yet, how about using just a single finger?

Upside down
If you really want to prove yourself, try playing a game with your controller the wrong way up. Relearning where all the buttons are might take a while, though!

Different peripherals
An oldie, but a goodie. If you want to impress your friends try playing your favorite games with weird accessories. It's great for keeping people guessing!

Blindfolded
The ultimate test of muscle memory and dexterity. This one requires you to learn an entire game so well that you can play it with your eyes closed.

Multiple players
Most games were designed to make use of your own hand-eye coordination. Get multiple people wrapped around the same controller and you'll need amazing communication skills to make the game work.

RACING GAMES

★ **START YOUR ENGINES!**

Few genres suit world records more than racing games. They're all about the fastest, the bravest, and the best! Racing games have been around almost as long as video games themselves, and even when they were little more than white blocks speeding up a road made out of lines, gamers around the world feverishly competed to see who could be the fastest of them all.

Nowadays, we have all sorts of amazing racers, from arcade fun like *Mario Kart 8* all the way up to the high-detailed simulations like *Assetto Corsa* and *Project Cars*. One thing's for certain though: whether you're cruising down Rainbow Road or trying to hit that perfect chicane in a sports car, everyone likes to go fast, and everyone likes to beat their friends! Maybe these amazing feats will inspire you to get even quicker!

Endurance and focus are needed in racing games—make every lap time count!

Did You Know?
The first racing game was called *Speed Race*. It was designed by the man who made *Space Invaders*, and came out over 40 years ago!

THE BIGGEST NUMBERS!

IT'S A WII, MARIO!

Mario Kart Wii sold an insane number of copies. In fact, **35.2 million** have been sold worldwide, making it the biggest racing game of all time, and easily the most popular *Mario Kart*. However, many say it's one of the weaker entries in the series—there are too many random elements for serious record breakers!

MOST ENTRIES IN A SERIES

The *Need for Speed* series has been around since 1994, and now features **22 entries**! There are three games with the name "Hot Pursuit", a story-driven action game called *The Run*, and the most recent is *Payback*. This expands on *The Run's* story-led design, with cool chases, set-pieces, and epic street racing!

MOST CARS

The superb *Forza Motorsport 7* on Xbox One features a staggering 700 cars! If you were to drive a different car every day, that would last you nearly two whole years! And with all sorts of tuning options and custom decals, that is a crazy amount of content, although it still trails its Sony counterpart, *Gran Turismo*, in this regard—*GT6* featured almost **1,200 cars** in total, the most ever seen in a racing game!

MOST CARS IN ONE RACE!

Perhaps you thought 30-plus vehicles in *F-Zero GX* was big? Well how about **20,000 cars** in one single *Trackmania* race. Yes, you read that correctly. 20,000! An amazing video by L4Bomb4 shows what happens when that many cars coexist on a single track.

MOST EXPENSIVE RARE RACING GAME

The ultra rare *BMX Airmaster* on the ancient Atari 2600 is one of the most expensive racing games today. Despite not actually being very good, it still sells for **over $200** to collectors—you won't find many racing games that fetch more.

VIRTUAL INSANITY

Racing games are changing, and in the future we will see way more virtual reality used in digital driving. Right now, games like *Project Cars*, *Dirt Rally* and *Driveclub* have seen virtual reality modes added, and *Gran Turismo Sport* was VR ready when it was released. High-level players say it's far easier to get great lap times in VR, thanks to the use of 3-D and the ability to perfectly judge corners. As long as it doesn't make you feel too nauseated!

❖ ❖ INCREDIBLE FEATS!

THE NEED FOR SPEED

SPEEDRUNNERS
FULL GAME COMPLETION (EASY MODE)
14m 59s

Technically it doesn't have any vehicles in it, but it is a game all about crossing the finish line ahead of your competitors, so it's still racing! It's also excellent, having wowed PC players for over a year and now enjoying a new lease of life on Xbox One. Somehow, TehSeven has managed to complete the entire game in under 15 minutes, clocking an almighty 14 minutes 59 seconds in his run through Easy mode.

EXCITEBIKE
SELECTION A FULL COMPLETION
5m 41s 36ms

An oldie, but still a goodie. A lot of younger gamers have actually been able to enjoy *ExciteBike* since it was released for free on Wii U Virtual Console, but it's very unlikely they'll be able to beat Andrewg for pace. His incredible 5m 41s for Selection A is a full 15 seconds faster than the second best time. Sometimes, those simple old-school game mechanics make for the most tight and technical speedruns.

MARIO KART 64
ALL CUPS
38m 42s 180ms

If you haven't seen how far great players can push the limits in a racing game, check out Abney 317. He does things that seem impossible, and his *Mario Kart 64* skills will blow your mind. This run through all the game's cups is a feat of near superhuman gaming skill. And he even talks while he's doing it!

F-ZERO BIG BLUE
FASTEST LAP
24.6s

One of the most memorable courses in any racer is the *F-Zero* classic, Big Blue, almost entirely due to its amazing music. One person who'll probably never get that tune out of his head is Hector T T Rodriguez, whose time of 24.6 seconds from back in 2009 is so good, even Captain Falcon couldn't beat it!

BURNOUT 2
POINT OF IMPACT
ALL CHAMPIONSHIPS
1hr 8m 49s

Back in the heyday of the Gamecube, you couldn't ask for a purer arcade racer than the brilliant *Burnout 2: Point Of Impact*. Here, NoLoveDeepWeb smashes through the entire game in just over an hour, chaining boosts almost non-stop and proving himself to be the best *Burnout 2* player. He may not be racing real-life opponents, but in many ways, this is even harder.

MARIO KART 8
MARIO STADIUM FASTEST LAP
1m 48s 106ms

Now here's a challenge for you. The fastest time on Mario Stadium in *Mario Kart 8* is definitely within reach for an experienced player—all you'd need to do is verify it and you could become a world record holder. Andrew Carrick's current time of 1:48.106 is respectable, but considering the ghost record on *Mario Kart 8 Deluxe* on Switch is under 1:41, it's an achievable goal. You can do it!

8 TOP TIPS
HOW TO BREAK RECORDS

GETTING AHEAD OF THE PACK

1 STUDY THE RACING LINE

It sounds simple, but if you don't know and follow the ideal racing line for every track, you're never going to be able to beat your friends' times, let alone the world's best. A lot of serious driving games have the racing line burnt into the track—games like *Forza* allow you to use an artificial one to help you.

2 FIGURE OUT THE HANDLING

Is it a drift-based car or one that grips the road? Four or two-wheel drive? Can it jump, or do you need 100% concentration like a rally vehicle? Make sure you know the exact capabilities of your car before you embark on your record-beating run.

4 STREAM!

Streaming is a great way to learn, but check your parents are OK with it first. Streaming your runs in front of an audience can be daunting, but you might just get some amazing advice from the racing game community, and make some friends along the way.

5 STUDY VIDEOS

If you're struggling to beat the best times, watching great runs on YouTube will help hugely. You will be able to see exactly when to brake, learn how hard to steer, and check the best racing lines. Then it's up to you to shave a few milliseconds off! Some games even have their own in-game replay systems tied to leaderboards, making it even easier to see where time can be saved.

3 PICK ONE GAME AND STICK WITH IT

It might be tempting to play a variety of racing games because there are so many great ones out there, but if you seriously want to break records, you're going to have to focus your efforts into one game and learn everything about it. Do you have the discipline to be great?

7 TIME TRIAL!

Practice time is always a good investment. All good racing games have a time trial mode, and that is how you will create the muscle memory that will lead to the best times. It'll help your overall racing skill, too!

6 USE A HIGH REFRESH MONITOR

Playing on a giant HDTV may look great, but you will always be at a disadvantage to those with high-refresh monitors. They let players have the best possible response times, so every decision they make is instantly represented on screen.

8 GET A WHEEL

Unless you're playing an arcade-style racer, you need a good wheel and pedals if you're going to really challenge the world's best drivers. It's expensive, though, so start saving your pennies!

TRAINING GAMES

GRAN TURISMO 6

The grandaddy of racing sims, *Gran Turismo* is the place to start if you want to perfect the arts of racing lines and apex cornering. If you can master a track in GT, you can master it anywhere.

BURNOUT PARADISE

Now this is all about speed and reactions. What better way to test your gaming skill than by flying down the road at 200mph (320 km/h), narrowly avoiding traffic and other racers?

MARIO KART 8 DELUXE

The best way to practice drifting and a great way to teach yourself to be calm under pressure. You may be good, but are you good when Bowser is hurling red shells at you?

DiRT 4

It's all about precision and speed in rally driving, and *DiRT 4* will push you to the limits of both, whether you're playing on a controller or using a steering wheel. A great teaching tool for all high-level racing games.

LONGEST STANDING RECORDS

HIGH SCORES THAT REALLY STOOD THE TEST OF TIME!

DONKEY KONG (ARCADE)

SCORE: 874,300
SET: 1982
BEATEN? YES (2000)

The tug-of-war for this game's crown has always been heated (there's a documentary about it, called *The King of Kong*), but Billy Mitchell's original record stood for a staggering 18 years before being topped. The game hits a "kill screen" on the 22nd loop of levels, meaning there are realistically only a finite number of points. For this reason, Wes Copeland's current record of 1,218,000 is considered to be close to a perfect game.

DRAGSTER (ATARI 2600)

SCORE: 5.51 SEC
SET: 1982
BEATEN? NO

This is a contentious one, as there's no evidence that this record-breaking time was achieved—it was set in private and hasn't even been *tied* in 35 years. Recently, experts picked apart the code and concluded that 5.57 was the fastest time physically possible, while the quickest recorded times behind Todd Rogers's ancient record on the Twin Galaxies platform come in at 5.61. If the record *is* legitimate (it's still acknowledged by Twin Galaxies), it seems likely that it was set on a prototype cartridge or made use of some kind of as-yet unreplicated beneficial bug, as 5.51 is by all accounts (bar one) unachievable.

STAR FIRE (ARCADE)

SCORE: 9,780
SET: 1982
BEATEN? NO

It's surprising that some of the all-time classics on this list had a single player dominate for so long. But in this case, it's not difficult to see why there haven't been many challengers to Laura Curran's top score—the game has aged horribly. That doesn't stop the score from being impressive, of course, especially when scoring is so low in the game. It would have taken an epic session to rack up that many points, and it seems nobody is willing to put in the time to challenge what is generally recognized as gaming's oldest current world record.

ASTEROIDS (ARCADE)

SCORE: 41,336,440
SET: 1982
BEATEN?
YES (2010)

The most impressive part of this record is that its holder, Scott Safran, was only 15 years old when he set it. He played for three days straight, accruing extra lives in order to leave the game idle while taking quick food and bathroom breaks. It took almost 30 years for someone to beat Safran's record, but that's exactly what John McAllister did in 2010 with a 58-hour run of his own, beating the score by "just" half a million points.

Did You Know?

Arcade shooter *Victory* also has a high score record dating back to 1982—a three-way tie for first, all with the maximum 999,999,999 points and all set within a month of one another!

SPACE INVADERS (ARCADE)

SCORE: 55,160
SET: 2003
BEATEN?
YES (2011)

Donald Hayes held the high score for the most famous arcade game (besides *Pac-Man*) for over eight years before it was challenged. But when that competition came, it certainly did not come in peace. Arcade owner Richie Knucklez didn't just beat Hayes' score—he *destroyed* it. Knucklez doubled the record to 110,510 in October 2011, before more than trebling the former record with a ridiculous score of 184,870 the following month. Nobody has even come close to beating that huge score so far, with the closest contender still over 100,000 off it!

CHOPLIFTER (ARCADE)

SCORE: 1,781,000
SET: 1986
BEATEN?
NO

Charles Collins only has one credit on the Twin Galaxies leaderboards, but he sure made it count! Way back in June 1986, he set a verified record score on this classic Sega arcade game, and it seems to be genuinely untouchable. In fact, going by Twin Galaxies' rankings, this insane score is higher than every other recorded score below it *combined*! Even the best players struggle to go much higher than half a million points due to how the difficulty ramps up on each new cycle, so it's unlikely Collins's score will ever be knocked from the top spot . . .

FIGHTING GAMES

Nothing beats the purity of a great one-on-one fighter. It all comes down to skill and execution, prediction and reaction—players that truly master their beat-'em-up of choice have an answer for more or less everything. That's the level of skill you'll need to work toward if you're looking to set fighting game records, and reaching it will take dedication.

Since the release of *Street Fighter IV* revived the competitive fighting scene a decade ago, both 2-D and 3-D fighters have made a real comeback—they're now among the most popular types of game both to play and to watch, as the skill level on display from pro players is truly astonishing! Do you have what it takes to go toe-to-toe with the best brawlers in the world?

🏆 THE BIGGEST NUMBERS!

THE ULTIMATE LIBRARY

In 2013, US gamer Paul Kownacki laid claim to the record for having the largest collection of fighting games. He had **244 unique games**, but updated his submission three years later to a still-uncontested **310 titles**, ranging from NES classics to recent PS3 brawlers. Will anybody step up to show off even more?

A SMASHING SUCCESS

The best-selling fighting franchise of all time is Nintendo's *Super Smash Bros.* series. It has sold more than **38 million** copies, with each of the five games contributing at least five million to that total. It's a close race, though—*Tekken* and *Street Fighter* are only just behind *Smash Bros.*, with total sales of 35 million and 34 million respectively.

DO THE EVOLUTION

EVO is the biggest tournament for fighting games, attracting thousands of the world's best players to compete every year. Since 1996, the event has dished out over **$1 million** in prize money, and EVO 2016 smashed all records when it attracted over **14,000 competitors** across nine games. *Street Fighter* is typically the headline game, although *Smash Bros.* is almost as popular—*Super Smash Bros. Melee* is still being played competitively over 16 years after it first released for GameCube!

SPOILED FOR CHOICE

There are plenty of fighting games with huge rosters, but the biggest of the lot isn't what you might think. Dwarfing the character rosters of *Marvel Vs. Capcom 2* (56) and *Tekken Tag Tournament 2* (59) is the superb Japan-only sequel *Tobal 2*, with a ridiculous **200 playable characters**. This includes all of the monsters from the RPG-like Quest Mode!

MY FIGHT MONEY!

The rarest fighting game around is the European release of *Kizuna Encounter* for Neo-Geo. The Japanese version is fairly common, but this European version is a lot more expensive—only a handful have ever gone up for sale and it typically goes for **over $10,000**! Collectors estimate that there could be as few as 15 copies out there.

THE CRAZIEST FIGHTERS EVER

WEIRD WARRIORS!

FIGHTERS MEGAMIX
This Sega Saturn oddity lets you pit the car from *Daytona* against the palm tree from developer AM2's logo. It's the strangest fight ever!

RAKUGA KIDS
Every fighter is a drawing brought to life, leading to incredibly inventive designs such as Marsa the chicken witch and the loveable Beartank.

GUILTY GEAR XRD
Sack-headed freakish doctor Faust is one of the all-time greats, but shout-outs to the mechanical masterpiece that is Bedman, too!

SKULLGIRLS
Everything from hair-based attacks to vintage cartoon villains are on show, but our favorite character is walking brass section, Big Band.

INCREDIBLE FEATS!

NOW, FIGHT A NEW RIVAL!

THE WINS DON'T STOP
When it comes to *Street Fighter* win streaks, **Ryan Hart** is the man to beat. He's been around on the pro circuit almost since it began, and has since been recognized for his achievements with several Guinness world records—"Most International Fighting Video Game Competition Wins," the longest win streak in *Street Fighter IV* (he defeated **169 players in a row** in 2010), and most consecutive opponents in *Street Fighter V.* He's too good!

CLASH OF THE CENTURY
Street Fighter V hides a valuable Trophy behind the hardest level of its Survival mode. To clear this, you'll need to **beat 100 consecutive opponents** with just a single life bar! Fortunately, you can invest points in health recovery or other buffs, but it's still extremely tough. So tough, in fact, that only **0.2% of players** on the PS4 version have managed it.

FIGHTING FIT
Thought Kinect and EyeToy were the only gaming devices to offer full body-tracking motion control? Think again! Sega released the Activator peripheral for the Genesis in 1993, an octagonal bank of light beams that players would stand in, punching and kicking to break the beams and trigger in-game attacks. Playing fighting games with this device was completely impractical, although it wasn't a complete bust—an enhanced version of the tech was used in arcade fighter *Dragon Ball Z V.R.V.S.* to great effect, making it **the first successful controller-free fighting game**!

THE BEAST IS UNLEASHED

Street Fighter pro Daigo Umehara stunned the world at EVO 2004 by doing the seemingly impossible—clutching victory from the jaws of defeat by **parrying all 15 hits** of Justin Wong's Chun-Li super in *Street Fighter III* and answering with his own combo to take the round as the entire room exploded into deafening cheers. This epic piece of play is now known as "EVO Moment 37," and is **one of the most famous feats in the history of eSports**. Go watch it for yourselves!

FIREBALL FRENZY

Ultra Street Fighter II's new fireball-chucking mini-game is little more than a novelty, but that hasn't stopped speedsters from acing the bonus mode in record time—Kodyurem is the **master of Way of the Hado** mode at the time of writing, beating the Expert level in just **41 seconds**. Kodyurem also has the records for both Beginner and Standard difficulties, too, at 19 and 23 seconds respectively.

WAY OF THE WARRIOR

Some sources cite 1976 release *Heavyweight Champ* as **the first fighting game**, although we'd argue that being based on boxing actually makes it a sports game. So, by this logic, the earliest fighting game would be **1979's *Warrior***—a top-down dueling game where two knights do battle. It used basic vector graphics projected onto a static backdrop, making it quite impressive for its time. Unfortunately, the machines were poorly constructed, meaning very few working units still exist today.

BRUTE FORCE

Tekken has always been best-in-class when it comes to bonus game modes, and these see a surprising amount of competitive play. Using the super-powerful True Ogre, Shirdel was able to get through *Tekken 3*'s side-scrolling Tekken Force mode in just **4m 50s**, almost three minutes quicker than the next best time! That's on Medium difficulty, too—dropping down to Easy allowed Shirdel to shave off yet another 30 seconds.

ActRaiser is a really interesting speedrun as it encompasses several very different styles of gameplay—side-scrolling action, real-time strategy, and world-building. Most speedruns only require one specific gaming skill set, but this SNES favorite tests three different disciplines.

It's considered by many to be among the hardest games ever, but that doesn't mean that *Battletoads* can't be tamed! It's no surprise to see TheMexicanRunner at the top of the game's leaderboard, though—he recently finished playing through every single NES game live on his Twitch channel. Wow!

RECORDS ROUND-UP

THE BEST OF THE REST! HOW CLOSE CAN YOU GET TO THESE EPIC TIMES?

M ost records featured here use the "Any%" category—the fastest route from the start to the end of the game. In cases where games feature exploits that can save crazy amounts of time, the "Any% Glitchless" record (or equivalent) has been used instead, in order to give a better idea of the fastest times without breaking the game!

TITLE	FORMAT	TIME	RUNNER
1001 Spikes	Various	00:17:15	Berumondo
ActRaiser	SNES	00:59:36	LeHulk
Advance Wars	GBA	01:13:24	Alistair Grant
Alex Kidd in Miracle World	Master System	00:11:43	KrazyRasmus
Another World	Various	00:11:12	xXmotsiXx
Ape Escape	PS1	00:45:02	eednob
Arms	Switch	00:19:51	Mileve
Axiom Verge	Various	00:34:57	Zecks
Banjo-Kazooie	N64	01:14:21	Jctomo
Banjo-Tooie	N64	02:42:40	Pjii
Bastion	Various	00:13:24	valentinoIAN
Battleblock Theater	Various	01:17:28	GameguySD
Battletoads	NES	00:12:45	TheMexicanRunner
Beyond Good & Evil	Various	02:22:45	Keanu23898
Billy Hatcher and the Giant Egg	GameCube	01:02:48	Squid
Breath of Fire III	PS1	08:18:02	Zheal
Captain Toad: Treasure Tracker	Wii U	01:18:36	Vallu
Castle Crashers	Various	01:11:26	soxdye9
Castlevania	NES	00:11:32	kmac
Castlevania II: Simon's Quest	NES	00:37:55	Burb
Castlevania: Aria of Sorrow	GBA	00:34:44	VB
Castlevania: Symphony of the Night	PS1	00:33:11	Dr4gonBlitz
Chrono Trigger	SNES	02:48:43	Redslash
Chocobo Racing	PS1	00:17:07	pogyo
Clue	Various	00:00:01	Chrno
Clustertruck	Various	00:18:56	097Aceofspades
Crash Bandicoot	PS1	00:40:55	Kojiroctr
Crash Bandicoot 2: Cortex Strikes Back	PS1	00:40:02	stuart0000
Crash Bandicoot 3: Warped	PS1	00:44:35	Kojiroctr
Crash Team Racing	PS1	00:50:47	Pull
Croc: Legend of the Gobbos	Various	00:33:49	Bobslej
Crusader of Centy	Genesis	00:43:23	geurge
Day of the Tentacle	Various	00:18:21	madmonkeymud
Diddy Kong Racing	N64	00:39:51	MrsGizamaluke
Donkey Kong 64	N64	02:05:42	Kiwikiller67
Donkey Kong Country	SNES	00:32:19	Pichi
Donkey Kong Country 2: Diddy's Kong Quest	SNES	00:39:49	V0oid

Clustertruck is a game built for speedrunning, but muscle memory alone will only get you so far. Modifiers, such as increased or reduced gravity or speed, radically change the way each level is played, and the developers have been known to alter these settings on-the-fly to mess with streamers!

PERFORMING FOR YOU

In the case of *Donkey Kong 64*, the very best times come in over an hour and a half quicker than this run, using crazy glitches to skip entire worlds, get skills early, and even do levels in completely the wrong order. Kiwikiller67 also holds the record in this category, with an amazing time of 00:26:09.

High-level play of *Freedom Planet* is amazing to watch, with experts stringing together complex combinations of moves to get around levels at an unbelievable pace. It's quite similar to the *Sonic* games, so might be something worth looking into if you're a fan of Sega's speedy mascot.

Given that you can run straight to Hyrule Castle from the start if you're brave enough, it's no surprise that *Breath of the Wild* is one of the quickest *Zelda* speedruns. The game is *much* more difficult this way, however, even though players can scan amiibo that give them bonus items to help reach the end quicker.

TITLE	FORMAT	TIME	RUNNER
Donkey Kong Country 3: Dixie Kong's Double Trouble	SNES	00:47:03	Sui_MinD
Donkey Kong Country: Tropical Freeze	Wii U	01:12:41	DKS
Donkey Kong Jr.	NES	00:01:29	jeffsledge
Dragon Quest VIII: Journey of the Cursed King	PS2	11:46:41	glasnonck
DuckTales	NES	00:07:13	Frippen87
Dust: An Elysian Tail	Various	00:46:56	FinnSpire
EarthBound	SNES	03:47:41	Ultimolce
Excitebike	NES	00:05:41	andrewg
Fez	Various	00:26:54	TGH
Final Fantasy VI	SNES	04:43:59	LCC
Final Fantasy VII	PS1	07:18:53	Luzbelheim
Final Fantasy VIII	PS1	08:26:07	Luzbelheim
Final Fantasy IX	PS1	08:49:34	Luzbelheim
Final Fantasy X	PS2	10:16:05	CaracarnVi
Final Fantasy X-2	PS2	03:41:49	CaracarnVi
Final Fantasy XII	PS2	05:52:46	roostalol
Final Fantasy XIII	Various	04:54:36	LewdDolphin21
Final Fantasy XV	Various	04:45:45	Ranmaru
Fire Emblem: Awakening	3DS	00:35:04	Yukiya
Freedom Planet	Various	00:30:38	Fladervy
Front Mission 3	PS1	05:42:57	Aether
Gauntlet	NES	00:15:30	Guggensulli
Golden Axe	Genesis	00:08:07	beadle111
Gunstar Heroes	Genesis	00:33:39	d4gr0n
Ico	PS2	00:56:30	Benko
Jak & Daxter: The Precursor Legacy	PS2	01:02:52	OutrageousJosh
Kingdom Hearts	PS2	05:24:21	Sonicshadowsilver2
Kingdom Hearts II	PS2	04:38:27	Ninten866
Kirby Air Ride	GameCube	00:19:14	yokaze
Kirby: Planet Robobot	3DS	01:42:59	yosshiV3
Kirby: Triple Deluxe	3DS	01:58:05	yosshiV3
Kirby's Adventure	NES	00:44:38	race_out
Kirby's Dream Land	Game Boy	00:11:20	jumpypenguin
Kirby's Epic Yarn	Wii	01:30:46	Paperario
The Legend of Zelda	NES	00:28:43	lackattack24
The Legend of Zelda: A Link to the Past	SNES	01:23:19	Xelna
The Legend of Zelda: Breath of the Wild	Switch	00:39:35	Orcastraw

TITLE	FORMAT	TIME	RUNNER
The Legend of Zelda: Link's Awakening	Game Boy	00:45:53	zmaster91
The Legend of Zelda: Majora's Mask	N64	02:47:08	TrevPerson
The Legend of Zelda: Ocarina of Time	N64	03:35:29	dannyb21892
The Legend of Zelda: Skyward Sword	Wii	04:59:41	gymnast86
The Legend of Zelda: Wind Waker	GameCube	03:55:44	ChaoticAce
LEGO Star Wars: The Complete Saga	Various	03:19:53	TSG
LittleBigPlanet	PS3	00:53:36	RbdJellyfish
Luigi's Mansion	GameCube	00:56:51	Snap
Luigi's Mansion: Dark Moon	3DS	03:05:28	RiiDOLSK
Mario Kart 8	Wii U	01:18:23	Leo_oo
Mega Man	NES	00:18:24	COOLKID
Mega Man 2	NES	00:26:49	ellonija
Mega Man X	SNES	00:31:13	Akiteru
Metroid	NES	00:11:49	MetroidMcFly
Metroid Fusion	GBA	01:12:52	JRP2234
Metroid Prime	GameCube	00:53:00	JustinDM
Metroid: Zero Mission	GBA	00:26:19	Eagle
Minecraft	Various	00:07:16	TheeSizzler
Monster Hunter 3 Ultimate	3DS	02:59:13	Kanata64
Monster Hunter Generations	3DS	03:06:05	greengatea
New Super Mario Bros.	Various	00:23:32	MyLittleWalrus
New Super Mario Bros. U	Wii U	00:39:22	Stache
NiGHTS into Dreams	Saturn	00:24:16	Claris
Octodad: Dadliest Catch	Various	00:18:06	misskaddykins
Okami	Various	03:44:43	IEternalDarkness
Ori and the Blind Forest	Various	00:22:34	Ikewolf
Owlboy	PC	01:39:06	ViresMajores
Pac-Man World	PS1	00:30:43	Joester98
Paper Mario	N64	01:43:05	imglower
Pikmin	GameCube	00:57:52	ild01
Pikmin 2	GameCube	01:45:45	keisen
Pikmin 3	Wii U	00:50:26	IceCube
Plants Vs. Zombies	Various	03:49:56	A1Major
Pokémon Black/White	DS	03:18:55	Sinstar
Pokémon Black 2/White 2	DS	03:15:22	werster
Pokémon Diamond/Pearl	DS	03:44:14	crafted
Pokémon Gold/Silver	Game Boy	03:18:41	Gunnermaniac3

Thanks to seeded runs where everything is in the same place every time, *Minecraft* has proven extremely popular as a speed game. Across its many categories, fans are always on the lookout for a seed that will give them the resources they need to reach the End and slay the dragon in record time!

While relatively easy to play at a casual level, *Ori and the Blind Forest* has a sky-high skill ceiling when it comes to movement techniques. Watch the best players leap, clamber, and soar over and around obstacles in ways you'd never have imagined . . . it's truly a sight to behold!

Every *Pokémon* game has a huge speedrunning community, but the nostalgia for the original *Red and Blue* makes them among the most popular. While the Any% category was retired, some remaining categories still make use of similar tricks to catch them all in a matter of minutes.

Sonic Adventure 2 remains one of the most popular games of its time with speedrunners. It requires skill in multiple genres to perform well. This makes runs exciting to both play and watch . . . except the grueling 180 Emblem category, which only one player has managed to finish in under ten hours!

TITLE	FORMAT	TIME	RUNNER
Pokémon Red/Blue	Game Boy	01:48:49	Exarion
Pokémon Ruby/Sapphire	GBA	02:03:15	Keizaron
Pokémon Snap	N64	00:20:52	Lvon117
Pokémon Sun/Moon	3DS	05:13:13	itotaka1031
Pokémon X/Y	3DS	03:45:30	GarfieldTheLightning
Pokémon Yellow	Game Boy	01:55:49	Gunnermaniac3
Portal	Various	00:16:03	097Aceofspades
Portal 2	Various	01:03:58	PerOculos
Ratchet & Clank	PS4	00:39:04	IAAA9362
Rayman	Various	01:14:10	Thextera
Rhythm Heaven Fever	Wii	01:15:47	Coldeggman
Rocket Knight Adventures	Genesis	00:27:44	vorpal
Rogue Legacy	Various	00:12:39	Poahr
Secret of Mana	SNES	03:57:01	Yagamoth
Shadow of the Colossus	PS2	01:27:55	Neurotaku
Shantae: Half-Genie Hero	Various	00:57:02	Tky619
Shenmue	Dreamcast	07:52:19	puri_puri
Shenmue II	Various	04:29:02	SeductiveSpatula
Shovel Knight	Various	00:42:51	Smaugy
The Simpsons Game	Various	01:19:41	GoldenBalloon
Skies Of Arcadia: Legends	GameCube	12:55:00	ngBurns
Sonic Adventure 2 Battle	Various	00:34:53	Darkpr0
Sonic CD	Sega CD	00:11:29	werster
Sonic Colors	Wii	00:58:48	CriticalCyd
Sonic Generations	Various	00:54:47	thebluemania
Sonic R	Saturn	00:06:10	daily
Sonic the Hedgehog	Genesis	00:10:53	Tenebrae
Sonic the Hedgehog 2	Genesis	00:14:58	mike89
Splatoon	Wii U	00:51:19	MoveFishGetOutTheWay
Spyro The Dragon	PS1	00:38:51	Touval
Star Fox 64	N64	00:22:24	Hayate
Star Fox Adventures	GameCube	05:11:06	JubJub62
StarTropics	NES	01:04:17	Foulco
SteamWorld Dig	Various	00:22:45	anxest
Street Fighter II	Various	00:09:47	cutelittlecow
Streets of Rage	Genesis	00:25:42	TSky
Strider	Arcade	00:08:15	Old School Gamer
Super Castlevania IV	SNES	00:31:47	FuriousPaul
Super Mario 3D Land	3DS	00:55:08	ZeldaCubed
Super Mario 3D World	Wii U	01:38:43	KingBoo
Super Mario 64	N64	00:47:56	cheese05

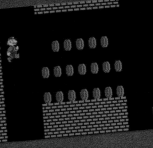

TITLE	FORMAT	TIME	RUNNER
Super Mario Bros.	NES	00:04:56	darbian
Super Mario Bros. 2	NES	00:08:26	IluvMario
Super Mario Bros. 3	NES	00:10:47	mfp
Super Mario Galaxy	Wii	02:34:26	Vallu
Super Mario Galaxy 2	Wii	03:01:57	Vallu
Super Mario Kart	SNES	00:35:16	dan_^h
Super Mario Land	Game Boy	00:12:25	callumbal
Super Mario RPG: Legend of the Seven Stars	SNES	02:49:13	Albrecht
Super Mario Sunshine	GameCube	01:14:40	nindeddeh
Super Mario World	SNES	00:09:45	Area51
Super Mario World 2: Yoshi's Island	SNES	01:42:57	Kolthor_TheBarbarian
Super Meat Boy	Various	00:17:41	Hamb
Super Metroid	SNES	00:41:56	Oatsngoats
Super Monkey Ball 2	GameCube	00:24:12	TheLostLlama
Super Paper Mario	Wii	04:23:31	imdead
Teslagrad	Various	00:20:42	MisterJack112
Titan Souls	Various	00:11:37	Scrublord
Tomb Raider	Various	01:47:47	redfooti
Tomb Raider II	Various	01:37:17	makeal
Trials Fusion	Various	00:39:41	iBlubbii
Trine	Various	00:32:30	MaximumLeech
Uncharted: Drake's Fortune	PS3	00:45:09	Mattmatt10111
Uncharted 2: Among Thieves	PS3	01:37:16	Mattmatt10111
Undertale	Various	01:04:26	tutelarfiber7
VVVVVV	Various	00:12:09	Chadwelli
WarioWare, Inc.: Mega Microgame$	GBA	00:29:43	werster
The Witness	Various	00:17:45	darkid
Xenoblade Chronicles	Wii	04:59:24	docmob
Yooka-Laylee	Various	00:24:32	TheRedSock
Yoshi's Woolly World	Wii U	02:24:51	be_be_be_
Zelda II: The Adventure Of Link	NES	00:54:12	Simpoldood

Watching darbian's astounding *Super Mario Bros.* run is watching both a game and player performance pushed to their very limits. While he makes it look almost effortless, his precision and mastery of every last aspect of the game are a great example of what you can achieve with enough dedication.

Undertale's short length and branching systems make it one of the few RPG speedruns that can really be recommended for beginners. It can still be difficult, but there's a lot more room for error—imagine making a mistake ten hours into a *Final Fantasy* speedrun and having to start over!

GLOSSARY

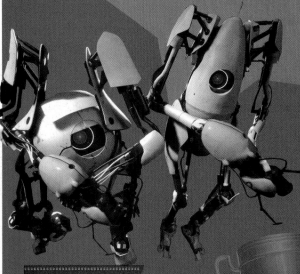

1CC
"One Credit Clear." Completing an arcade game that has a defined end point without using a continue—in almost all score record categories, the use of additional credits is prohibited. Not that it'd do you much good in a lot of cases, as using a continue often resets your high score anyway.

FRAMES

The individual rendered images that make up a game's graphics. For a game running at 60 frames per second (fps), the image is updated 60 times per second, giving fluid motion and better response times. However, it also calls for more precision—if something must be performed on a particular frame (known as it being a "frame perfect" trick) in a 60fps game, it needs to be done in an exact window of just 1/60th of a second!

ACE
"Arbitrary Code Execution," whereby specific and extremely precise strings of movement and actions allow the code of the game to be modified. Simpler examples (like skipping straight to the credits in early *Pokémon* games and *Super Mario World*) can be performed by hand by skilled players.

ANY%
A category of speedrun where the object is simply to get from the start of a game to the finish as quickly as possible. This category often uses various significant tricks, skips, and glitches, in order to shave off precious seconds.

GDQ
Biannual charity speedrun marathon Games Done Quick, where hundreds of the world's best players perform runs around the clock, for a full week. With over $13.8 million (£10 million) raised so far, it's the biggest event of the speedrunning calendar.

KILL SCREEN
Some old arcade games (including *Pac-Man* and *Donkey Kong*) reach a point where it becomes impossible to progress further, limiting the length of a session and the number of points up for grabs. This is known as a kill screen, as it kills the run.

LOW%
Speedruns where the object is to finish the game while avoiding as many power-ups, abilities, and upgrades as possible. Without these seemingly "essential"

powers, complex tricks are often needed to bypass obstacles—*Super Mario 64* usually requires 70 stars to reach the final level, but the most skilled players can now reach Bowser without grabbing a single star along the way!

OUT OF BOUNDS
Sometimes shortened to "OoB," this refers to any glitch or trick that leaves the intended play area via unintended means. OoB skips are banned in certain categories and games, as they can sometimes be used to completely break a game in a matter of minutes.

PRIZE POOL
The total amount of prize money up for grabs at a tournament or eSports event. The overall winner typically claims the lion's share of the cash, with the rest of the prize money divided between runners-up based on their position.

RNG
Random Number Generator, the part of a game's code used to determine how and when "random" events (like wild Pokémon battles or which attack a boss will use) will occur. In rare examples, RNG can be manipulated and exploited by performing certain strings of actions to achieve the same results every time.

RTA
A speedrun performed in real time, rather than recorded in individual segments. External timers are often used if the in-game clock is particularly vague (like in *Pokémon* games, which round to the nearest minute).

TAS
Tool-Assisted Speedruns, where external tools (such as frame advance and save state functions in emulators) and complex manipulation techniques are used to create optimal runs, often incorporating tricks so technical that they'd be all but impossible for a human player to replicate. Such tricks are referred to as "TAS-only."